PAINLESS
Writing

Jeffrey Strausser

illustrated by Denise Gilgannon

All inquiries should be addressed to:
Barron's Educational Series, Inc.
250 Wireless Boulevard
Hauppauge, New York 11788
http://www.barronseduc.com

Library of Congress Catalog Card No. 2001025130

International Standard Book No. 0-7641-1810-2

Library of Congress Cataloging-in-Publication Data

Strausser, Jeffrey.
      Painless writing / Jeffrey Strausser.
          p.   cm.
      Includes index.
      ISBN 0-7641-1810-2
      1. English language—Composition and exercises—Study and
teaching (Middle school)—Juvenile literature.   2. Report writing
—Juvenile literature.   [1. English language—Composition and
exercises.   2. Report writing.]   I. Title.
      LB1631 .S822 2001
      808'.042'0712—dc21   2001025130

PRINTED IN THE UNITED STATES OF AMERICA
9 8 7 6

CONTENTS

To Beth, Katie, and Matthew

INTRODUCTION

What this book will do for you

Many students admit that their writing detracts from their hard work, rather than complements it. They realize that when they write with an uninteresting and mechanical style, they compete at a disadvantage. Unfortunately, these students sometimes become confused about how to improve their faulty writing style. Does your writing hurt you? If you think that it does, can you improve your writing? Absolutely! Can you improve your writing quickly? Absolutely! However, you must know how to go about it.

Developing a good writing style is similar to learning to play a sport or a musical instrument because writing well also requires mastering specific techniques. Did you ever notice how great athletes and musicians make what they are doing look natural? Yet we know athletes and musicians must learn their specific skills. Similar to sports and music, writing improvement comes from first separating the techniques, then studying the techniques, and finally, permanently incorporating them into your writing style. This book presents powerful and easily applied techniques to make your writing clear, interesting, and concise. Employing these techniques will immediately transform your writing style so that you can write better with less time and effort—and your grades will improve as your writing improves.

The good news is that you will not need to memorize endless lists of vocabulary words, or diagram sentences, or conjugate verbs before you can make these techniques work for you. These focused techniques will require only a small amount of time to master.

This book explains nine Painless Techniques that will dramatically improve your writing. Each technique has its own chapter that describes and demonstrates the technique through straightforward examples. Practice makes permanent; each chapter contains writing exercises to help you make these techniques a permanent part of your writing style. Finally, for the Internet surfers, each chapter contains sections where you can surf through the Internet to read additional information about topics discussed in the chapter. It is not necessary to refer to these sites, as each Painless Technique is concisely but thoroughly explained within the pages of the chapter. However, if surfing through the ocean of cyberspace is fun for you, just look for the *Surf's up* box and check out the web pages listed there.

Does dramatically improving your writing and improving your grades appeal to you? If so, grab the reins and take control of your writing. It is never too late to develop a clear, interesting, and concise writing style. The sooner you begin, the sooner it will happen. It's painless!

Web Addresses Change!

You should be aware that addresses on the World Wide Web are constantly changing. While every attempt has been made to provide you with the most current addresses available, the nature of the Internet makes it virtually impossible to keep abreast of the many changes that seem to occur on a daily basis.

If you should come across a web address (URL) that no longer appears to be valid, either because the site no longer exists or because the address has changed, don't panic. Simply do a key word search on the subject matter in question. For example, if you are interested in finding out more about prepositional phrases and the particular address appears to be invalid, do a search for various words related to prepositional phrases. These are the key words. A key word search for this topic might include, for example, noun phrases. If an initial key word search provides too many potential sites, you can always narrow the number of choices by doing a second key word search that will limit your original search to only those sites that contain the terms from both your first and second searches.

WARNING: Not every response to your search will match your criteria, and some sites may contain adult material. If you are ever in doubt, check with someone who can help you.

CHAPTER ONE

Clean Up Preposition Clutter

PREPOSITION OVERUSE RUINS YOUR STYLE

Overusing prepositions and their accompanying phrases not only creates boring writing, but writing that is usually hard to understand. Let's see if we can figure out why this happens. Have you ever read something where the writer used too many words to describe what was happening or to describe something? Remember growing increasingly frustrated until you said, "Enough, already!" and started skimming, or worse yet, you just quit reading? Many times, a writer using multiword, vague prepositional phrases rather than one-word descriptive adjectives or prepositions causes wordy writing because he or she uses many words when only a few are needed. Unfortunately, the problems do not stop there because many students substitute prepositional phrases throughout their writing where verbs would have been the better choice. This writing fault leaves them with a passage that is now not only wordy, but also dull. This wordiness and dullness causes readers to skim, and once they begin skimming, they are not going to fully appreciate the work that you put into your assignment.

Look at some of your writing. Be honest. Is it wordy . . . dull . . . hard to understand? Maybe you are writing with too many wordy and vague prepositional phrases. If you are, don't worry! This common writing fault can be easily corrected. All you have to do is use the Painless Technique presented in this chapter and you will soon be

ELIMINATING UNNECESSARY PREPOSITIONAL PHRASES.

Don't use too much of a good thing

Do not eliminate all prepositions from your writing because prepositions and prepositional phrases are essential to writing. We need prepositions to communicate our ideas, but the problem is that many writers overuse them because dropping in preposition after preposition seems easier than trying to write concisely or find active verbs that keep the reader's interest. However, you will soon learn that this is not the case. Overusing prepositions is a common fault, which left unattended develops into a bad habit that leads to wordy and dull writing. Therefore, eliminate all *unnecessary* prepositions and their accompanying wordy baggage. The first Painless Technique will help you eliminate this dull baggage from your writing. Let's start by stating this first technique.

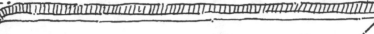

Painless Technique

PAINLESS TECHNIQUE NO. 1: MAKE YOUR WRITING CLEARER AND MORE INTERESTING BY ELIMINATING UNNECESSARY PREPOSITIONAL PHRASES.

IDENTIFYING PREPOSITIONS

Make sure you can identify prepositions and their phrases

A *preposition* is a word used to link a noun to a sentence, and in so doing, relates the noun to either another noun or a verb. Below are some common prepositions that we use all the time in our writing.

by	because
under	during
for	from
near	like
about	over
on	in
against	until
to	across
with	above
next	toward
inside	outside

A *prepositional phrase* consists of a preposition and a noun acting as the preposition's object. Within this phrase, the preposition depicts a relationship to the noun. Some prepositional phrases are shown below.

on the beach	*off* the cuff
near the desk	*during* his speech
against the wind	*across* the continent
from the beginning	*toward* the end
under the table	*until* the last

Surf's up...

If you want to check out the ocean of information available on identifying prepositions, a great site is

www.gabsicott.com/bigdog/prepositions.htm

Now that we can identify prepositions and their accompanying phrases, we have to ask

HOW MANY PREPOSITIONS ARE TOO MANY?

Unfortunately, there is no easy rule to apply that will clearly tell you whether you have overloaded your writing with prepositions. However, if your sentences contain only a few verbs, especially verbs in the passive voice, and many prepositions, your report or essay is probably wordy and confusing. (In Chapter Three we talk more about what happens to your writing when you use the passive voice.) Alternatively, if you are a numbers type person, a reasonable rule of thumb is that if your writing contains 20 percent to 25 percent prepositions, you probably have used too many prepositions.

Too many prepositions

Unnecessary prepositions and their wordy baggage, as well as passive voice sentences, riddle the following paragraphs. Notice how difficult the passage is to follow. Imagine several pages of this!

Exploring Mars

At this point in time, Mars is the target of the modern astronaut. By reason of its relative closeness to Earth, Mars is being studied by scientists for the purposes of a future mission. In a manner similar to the earlier study of the Moon by scientists, a probe is planned to be sent by NASA to within the immediate vicinity of the planet with a view toward collecting data with respect to the atmosphere of the planet. NASA plans to send in excess of one dozen of these probes during the course of the next five years.

From the point of view of a nonscientist, this proposed expenditure of billions of dollars for the purpose of studying an inhospitable planet appears to be a waste of money and human effort. At this point in time, our own planet and its inhabitants are in need of attention, particularly with regard to the environment. However, on the basis of what I have seen thus far, this concern will not be addressed at this point in time or at a point later into the future.

We must not succumb to this attack of viciousness on our common sense. Of course, I am writing in reference to the concerted effort of the community of scientists, the politicians, and the groups with special interests. We must persevere in our quest to bring this question of social importance to the attention of the public.

This essay is an extreme example of preposition overuse. Use the exercise below to see how the writer overuses prepositions and their accompanying phrases. Remember that any amount of preposition overuse puts you at risk of losing your reader's attention.

BRAIN TICKLERS
Set # 1

Underline the prepositions and their accompanying prepositional phrases in the *Exploring Mars* essay.

(Answers are on page 213.)

Beware of long sentences containing many prepositions

Wordiness and dullness can occur when you write with long, preposition-filled sentences because long sentences containing several prepositions and only a few verbs are nearly impossible to understand. Take another look at *Exploring Mars*, and this time notice the preposition-filled next-to-last sentence of the first paragraph. The writer makes the sentence even more difficult to read by making it a long sentence laced with unnecessary prepositions and their wordy baggage.

THE PREPOSITION-FILLED LONG SENTENCE

In a manner similar to the earlier study of the Moon by scientists, a probe is planned to be sent by NASA to within the immediate vicinity of the planet with a view toward collecting data with respect to the atmosphere of the planet.

The good writer strives to be clear, concise, and interesting, which means that long preposition-filled sentences such as this one will lose your reader's interest.

The real test is in the reading

The preposition-to-total-words ratio aside, the real test to determine whether you have used too many prepositions is in the reading. If you find yourself reading a dull passage, or skimming over words, perhaps the writing is suffering from preposition overload. As you become more aware of this common, and curable, writing fault, it will become second nature to you to look at your writing and ask yourself

<u>WILL ELIMINATING SOME PREPOSITIONS
IMPROVE THIS WRITING PIECE?</u>

If you suspect prepositions often clutter your writing, apply the technique of this chapter by using the following five-step process to reduce preposition clutter.

FIVE STEPS TO ELIMINATING UNNECESSARY PREPOSITIONS

Let's see how you can eliminate the unnecessary prepositions and their wordy baggage from your writing. We'll start by tackling one of the greatest causes of clutter and dullness: the compound prepositional phrase.

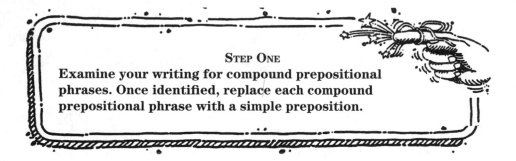

STEP ONE
Examine your writing for compound prepositional phrases. Once identified, replace each compound prepositional phrase with a simple preposition.

Identify and eliminate compound prepositional phrases

A *compound prepositional phrase* is a series of prepositional phrases that act like a single preposition. Many writers ignore simple, powerful prepositions such as *on* and *of*. Instead, they select wordy compound prepositional phrases because they think this makes the writing style appear more sophisticated. However, the opposite is true because it is the unsophisticated and lazy writer who opts for the compound prepositional phrases rather than taking time to select the proper verb and preposition.

Compound prepositional phrases are nothing but clutter

Below are some common compound prepositional phrases. As you read them, notice how they are formed.

> *with regard to = with regard + to*
> *with respect to = with respect + to*
> *in reference to = in reference + to*
> *in connection with = in connection + with*
> *for the purposes of = for the purposes + of*

A compound prepositional phrase begins with a complete prepositional phrase. However, it is a prepositional phrase that cannot stand alone so it must combine forces with another preposition just to link the noun to the sentence. Consequently, you fill the page with more words than you need to express your ideas. What is the solution to eliminating this type of wordiness? Convert compound prepositions to simpler prepositions, or eliminate the entire compound prepositional phrase. Below are some examples demonstrating how some wordy compound prepositions can be reduced to single-word prepositions or eliminated.

Convert the compound prepositions to simple prepositions or eliminate them

POOR

In order to write more concisely, eliminate compound prepositional phrases.

BETTER

To write more concisely, eliminate compound prepositional phrases.

Notice that by deleting the prepositional phrase, *in order*, we eliminated an unnecessary preposition and wordy baggage.

POOR

At this point in time, we are writing well.

BETTER

Now, we are writing well.

The wordy prepositional phrase, *at this point in time,* was eliminated and replaced with the single word expression, *now*.

POOR

These procedures are required *in accordance with* school policy.

BETTER

These procedures are required *by* school policy.

BETTER STILL

School policy requires these procedures.

The wordy compound prepositional phrase, *in accordance with*, is replaced by the single word preposition, *by*. Notice, however, that the sentence is still written in the passive voice. If you're a little confused about understanding the difference between active and passive voice, hang on and we'll discuss the difference shortly. For a detailed discussion, refer to Chapter Three. The last sentence uses the active voice and eliminates the preposition, *by*. Notice that the word count drops from nine words in the first sentence to five words in the active and direct last sentence.

POOR

I am writing *with reference to* the free ticket offer.

BETTER

I am writing *about* the free ticket offer.

Here, the compound prepositional phrase, *with reference to*, is replaced with the one word preposition, *about*.

Listed below are some common compound prepositional phrases and their simpler counterparts. Learn to recognize and replace the wordy compound prepositional phrase with the one-word preposition.

Compound Prepositional Phrase	Simple Preposition
at that point in time	then, now
by means of	by
by reason of	because of
by virtue of	by, under
during the course of	during
for the purposes of	for, under
from the point of view of	from, for
in accordance with	by, under
in a manner similar to	like
in excess of	more than, over
in favor of	for
in receipt of	having received
in relation to	about, concerning
in terms of	in
in the nature of	like
in the immediate vicinity of	near
in close proximity to	near
on the basis of	by, from
with a view to	to
with reference to	about, concerning
with regard to	about, concerning
with respect to	about, concerning

BRAIN TICKLERS
Set # 2

First, identify the compound prepositional phrases in each of the following sentences, then rewrite the sentences using concise, simple prepositions. The number in parentheses at the end of each sentence denotes the number of words in the sentence. Notice how many words you eliminate by replacing the compound prepositional phrase with a simple preposition.

1. The Smiths live in the immediate vicinity of our school. (10)

2. By virtue of winning the most games during the season, our team earned the home court advantage. (17)

3. At this point in time, we are not sure where we are going on vacation. (15)

4. During the course of our conversation, we decided not to spend in excess of ten dollars. (16)

5. He called me in reference to the new class that was forming. (12)

6. He ate in excess of six doughnuts. (7)

7. She is calling in relation to the swimming lessons. (9)

8. I am in favor of taking another class trip. (9)

9. Anna journeyed to Phoenix by means of car. (8)

10. I am in receipt of your letter. (7)

11. During the course of the class, I fell asleep. (9)

12. He won the contest by means of cheating. (8)

13. I live in the immediate vicinity of you. (8)

14. I am in receipt of your note. (7)

15. I have a question in relation to my final history grade. (11)

(Answers are on pages 213–214.)

Use participles to help eliminate unnecessary prepositions

Once you have eliminated all wordy compound prepositional phrases, you have done much to improve your writing submission. However, there are still four more steps in this technique to help you rid your writing of wordiness and dullness caused by preposition overuse. Step Two encourages you to examine your writing for prepositional phrases that can be converted into verb forms, known as participles.

A *participle* is a verbal form of a word, having the qualities of both verb and adjective. For this reason, we also refer to a participle as a *verbal adjective*. Notice how the participles below help convey a sense of action to your sentences.

> *Smiling* but silent, John left the room.
> *Crying*, the girls ran from the dance.

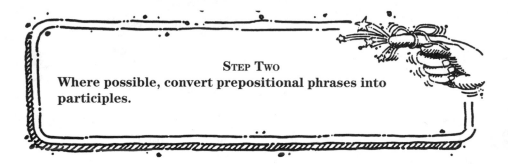

STEP TWO
Where possible, convert prepositional phrases into participles.

POOR

In the attempt to write a concise essay, he left out important facts.

BETTER

Attempting to write a concise essay, he left out important facts.

The above example shows how you can eliminate the four-word prepositional phrase, *in the attempt to*, with the one-word participle, *attempting*. The following example shows how you can eliminate two wordy prepositional phrases with one stroke.

POOR
In the fear of failure, he sought help with his English homework.

BETTER
Fearing failure, he sought help with his English homework.

Notice that not only does this step eliminate unnecessary words, but it also provides the revised sentence with a greater sense of action.

POOR
In response to the alarm, the fire truck hurtled down the street.

BETTER
Responding to the alarm, the fire truck hurtled down the street.

Here we have a compound preposition, *in response to*. The sentence can be improved by replacing this compound preposition with the participle, *responding*.

BRAIN TICKLERS
Set # 3

First, identify the prepositional phrase in each of the following sentences, then rewrite each sentence by converting the prepositional phrase to a participle form. Compare how your new sentence portrays more action, and is less wordy. Remember that the numbers in parentheses refer to the word count in each sentence.

1. With regard to my grade, the teacher was against changing it. (11)

2. With a sense of doom, he called for help. (9)

3. In his desire to do well in school, John quit playing baseball five days a week. (16)

4. In a race against time, Sally stayed up all night working on her project. (14)

5. With an eye on the storm clouds, the family unpacked the picnic basket. (13)

6. Without much concern, Sandy walked down the dimly lit street. (10)

7. In need of money, the students called home. (8)

8. In his hurry to paint the birdhouse, John spilled the paint. (11)

9. With a lack of common sense, the boys raced the train to the crossing. (14)

10. With his lack of manners, he embarrassed everyone seated at the dinner table. (13)

11. With the hope of landing a movie part, the young actor studied his lines. (14)

12. With a taste of victory, the runner bolted across the finish line. (12)

13. The student, with one eye on the clock, hurried through the test. (12)

(Answers are on pages 215–216.)

Squeeze action out of adverbs

Once you have transformed prepositional phrases into verb forms, where possible, investigate converting the remaining prepositions into adverbs. An *adverb* is a word that describes a verb, an adjective, or another adverb, and tells where, when, how, how often or how long, or how much. Because of the function of adverbs, when you replace prepositions with them, your writing creates a greater sense of action.

Below are some examples of commonly used adverbs:

The team won *easily*.
I *hardly* knew the teacher.
The cyclist hit the ground *hard*.
He arrived *late* for the play rehearsal.

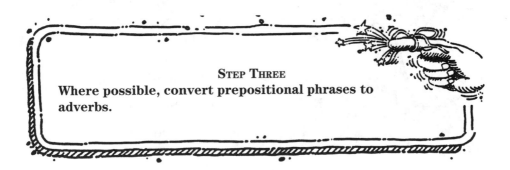

STEP THREE
Where possible, convert prepositional phrases to adverbs.

POOR
The writer's novels were *of critical acclaim*.

BETTER
The writer's novels were *critically acclaimed*.

Notice that converting the prepositional phrase, *of critical acclaim*, to an adverb phrase, *critically acclaimed*, creates a greater sense of action in the second sentence.

POOR
The patient's symptoms were *under close watch*.

BETTER
The patient's symptoms were *closely watched*.

In this example, the prepositional phrase, *under close watch*, transforms to an adverb phrase, *closely watched*. (Take note that this sentence remains in the passive voice.)

BRAIN TICKLERS
Set # 4

Identify the prepositional phrase in each of the following sentences, then rewrite each sentence by converting the prepositional phrase to an adverb. Notice how the new sentence portrays more action with fewer words.

1. His actions were under close control. (6)

2. Her books were under strict censure. (6)

3. His speech was comprised of many humble statements. (8)

4. John was the victim of a brutal attack. (8)

5. Janet was under the mistaken assumption that she was not liked. (11)

6. The senator's remarks were under intense scrutiny. (7)

(Answers are on page 216.)

Take advantage of the power of adjectives

An *adjective* is a word that describes a noun or pronoun and tells which one, what kind, or how many. Adjectives help your readers visualize your facts, characters, and point of view. The next step of the technique requires that, where possible, you convert the remaining unnecessary prepositions and their accompanying words to adjectives.

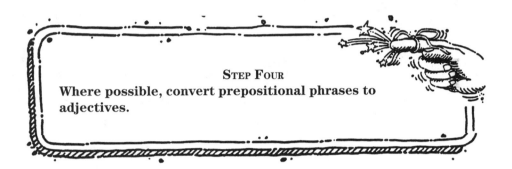

STEP FOUR
Where possible, convert prepositional phrases to adjectives.

POOR
It is the nature *of humans* to admire beauty.

BETTER
It is *human* nature to admire beauty.

Notice how converting the prepositional phrase, *of humans*, to an adjective makes the sentence read more smoothly.

POOR
The response *of the audience* was silence.

BETTER
The *audience's* response was silence.

By converting the prepositional phrase to an adjective, we add clarity to the new sentence, as well as reducing the number of words in the sentence.

BRAIN TICKLERS
Set # 5

Begin by identifying the prepositional phrase in each of the following sentences. Once selected, rewrite each sentence by converting the prepositional phrase to an adjective so that the revised sentence is less stilted and contains fewer words.

1. The loss of time will never be regained. (8)

2. John's manner of speaking bored the audience. (7)

3. The quarterback was the leader of the team. (8)

4. Nocturnal animals avoid the light of day. (7)

5. The famous adventurer now craved a life of calm. (9)

6. What to eat for lunch was the problem of the day. (11)

7. Living in a life of luxury had become second nature to the wealthy family. (14)

8. The response of the class to the teacher's joke was many groans. (12)

(Answers are on pages 216–217.)

Be active, not passive

After you have eliminated all compound prepositional phrases and, where possible, transformed prepositions and their associated words to verbs, adverbs, or adjectives, check your sentences to be sure they are written in the active voice, rather than the passive voice. Using unnecessary prepositions will often lead to passive voice sentences that are usually wordy, dull, and hard to understand. These problems occur because the subject in a passive voice sentence is acted upon, rather than doing the acting. This sentence structure removes the action and the directness from the sentence. Let's look at a better alternative to the passive voice: the active voice.

What is the active voice? Simply stated, when a sentence is written in the active voice, the subject of the sentence is the person or thing performing the action. This sentence structure creates a greater sense of action, and it does so with fewer words. For further explanation of the active versus the passive voice, refer to Chapter Three, which illustrates how to identify and transform passive voice sentences into active voice sentences. However, for now, an easy way to determine whether a sentence is in the passive voice is to ask yourself, "Who or what is performing the action?" Once you have identified the actor, make that person or thing the subject of your sentence, and then complement the subject with a verb that describes the action. Chapter Three also discusses other problems beside wordiness created by passive voice writing.

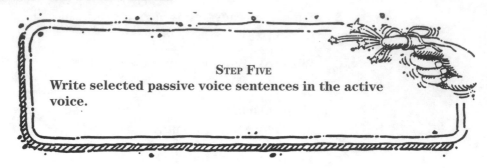

STEP FIVE
Write selected passive voice sentences in the active voice.

POOR

The exam scores were tabulated *by the teacher*.

BETTER

The *teacher* tabulated the exam scores.

In the first sentence, the subject (*exam scores*) was acted upon. This structure tells us the author has written the sentence in the passive voice. The revised sentence takes the noun contained in the prepositional phrase of the first sentence and converts it to a subject so that in the revised, active voice sentence, the subject, *teacher*, performs the action. Notice how the revised sentence eliminates the prepositional phrase, *by the teacher*, and how it conveys more action than the original passive voice sentence.

POOR

The baseball card was purchased *by the collector*.

BETTER

The *collector* purchased the baseball card.

In the first sentence, the subject, *baseball card*, was acted upon. As in the example above, this structure tells us the writer has written the sentence in the passive voice. The revised sentence makes the subject, *collector*, perform the action. Notice how the new sentence eliminates the prepositional phrase of the original sentence and subsequently conveys more action.

POOR

The witness's remarks were recorded *by the police officer*.

BETTER
The *police officer* recorded the witness's remarks.

In the first sentence, the subject, *witness's remarks*, was acted upon. The revised sentence eliminates the unnecessary prepositional phrase, *by the police officer*, thus making the sentence clearer and more direct.

BRAIN TICKLERS
Set # 6

Identify the prepositional phrase in the following sentences that result in the passive voice, then eliminate the unnecessary prepositional phrase and rewrite the sentences in the active voice. Notice how the sentences are more direct, as well as less wordy. The number in the parentheses at the end of the sentence is the number of words in the sentence. Use it to compare the number of words in your new sentence to the original passive sentence.

1. The teacher's instructions were misunderstood by the students. (8)

2. His success was resented by his teammates. (7)

3. The grocery store was operated under new management. (8)

4. The grounds were observed by means of hidden cameras. (9)

5. The last four games were lost by the team. (9)

6. The unusual plants were studied by the scientists. (8)

7. The touchdown pass was caught by the speedy receiver. (9)

8. The dance troupe was started by a world-renowned dancer. (10)

9. Their desire for adventure was tempered by the rough seas. (10)

(Answers are on pages 217–218.)

This five-step process should rid your writing of most unnecessarily used prepositions. Extreme preposition overuse may require changing the entire paragraph structure to apply the five-step process. For instance, you may need to chop a long sentence into two or three sentences, or convert several offending simple sentences into a concise compound sentence. Remember that you can always simply eliminate prepositions if they do not contribute to the meaning or action of the sentence.

APPLYING THE FIVE-STEP PROCESS

The following paragraph fulfills our criteria for excessive preposition use. The 70-word paragraph contains 14 prepositions yielding a preposition-to-total word ratio of 20 percent. Furthermore, it is dull reading. Let's rewrite this paragraph using this first technique's five-step process. The technique involves taking each sentence and working through each of the steps until we eliminate the unnecessary preposition(s) and their accompanying wordy baggage. Our goal is to finish with a passage that is less wordy and conveys a greater sense of action.

By virtue of learning to write better, you will open a whole new world *with reference to* career opportunities. It is *of importance* that students realize that writers will be needed *by* the education and business communities. *In the present,* both *of these sectors* have expressed disappointment *in the writing skills of those employed.* Make no mistake about it; people who can write well are demanded *by* employers everywhere.

Beginning with the first sentence:

POOR

By virtue of learning to write better, you will open a whole new world *with reference to* career opportunities.

First, *by virtue of* is a compound prepositional phrase that adds nothing to the sentence, and therefore we can eliminate this wordy phrase (Step One). Next, *with reference to* is a compound prepositional phrase that we can convert to the participle, *regarding* (Steps One and Two). Now, our new first sentence reads:

BETTER

Learning to write better will open a whole new world regarding career opportunities.

Moving to the second sentence:

POOR

It is *of importance* that students realize that writers will be needed *by* the education and business communities.

The prepositional phrase, *of importance*, can be converted to the one-word adjective, *important* (Step Four). Moreover, the sentence is in the wordy passive voice and should be rewritten into the active voice (Step Five). Let us include our Step Four change here and create a new second sentence:

BETTER

It is important that students realize that the education and business communities will need writers.

Next, sentence three:

POOR

In the present, both *of these sectors* have expressed disappointment *in the writing skills of those employed.*

The prepositional phrase, *in the present*, can be converted to the adverb, *presently* (Step Three). We can eliminate the unnecessary prepositional phrase, *of these sectors*, without changing the sentence's meaning. Further, we can combine the prepositional phrases, *in the writing skills* and *of those employed*, into the phrase, *their employees' writing skills*. Our new third sentence reads:

BETTER

Presently, both sectors have expressed disappointment in their employees' writing skills.

Now, on to the last sentence:

POOR

Make no mistake about it; people who can write well are demanded *by* employers everywhere.

We spot the preposition, *by*, and notice that the portion of the sentence following the semicolon is passive voice. If we rewrite this portion into the active voice, it will read:

> *employers everywhere are demanding people who can write well.*

Our last sentence is now:

BETTER

Make no mistake about it; employers everywhere are demanding people who can write well.

Now we are ready to inspect the rewritten paragraph.

Learning to write better will open a whole new world regarding career opportunities. It is important that students realize that the education and business communities will need writers. Presently, these sectors have expressed disappointment in their employees' writing skills. Make no mistake about it; employers everywhere are demanding people who can write well.

Our new excerpt conveys the same information, not only more clearly and forcefully, but also more concisely. The rewritten paragraph contains only 53 words, a 25 percent word reduction. The prepositions decreased from 14 to just 3, thereby creating a more clear and concise paragraph.

To review, the five-step process associated with this first technique is

Step One: Examine your writing for compound prepositional phrases. Once identified, replace each compound prepositional phrase with a simple preposition.

Step Two: Where possible, convert candidate prepositional phrases into participles.

Step Three: Where possible, convert candidate prepositional phrases into adverbs.

Step Four: Where possible, convert candidate prepositional phrases to adjectives.

Step Five: Write selected passive voice sentences in the active voice.

BRAIN TICKLERS
Set # 7

Transform the following wordy paragraphs into a clear and concise excerpt. Use Painless Technique No. 1's five-step process to minimize the paragraphs' prepositions in order to make the writing flow better and reduce its wordiness.

Out There

Pluto and Uranus take turns being the most distant planets in reference to the Sun. For years, scientists were under the mistaken hypothesis that Pluto was the most distant planet. Scientists, in an attempt to assimilate astronomical data, learned their hypothesis was inaccurate. Fortunately, it is of the scientists' nature to investigate all data. On the basis of the data, the astronomers learned of the fact that the two planets have intersecting orbits. In addition, during the course of their investigation, they learned much of the nature of the two planets.

The surface of both of these planets is known to be cold because of their lack of atmosphere and their position with reference to the Sun. It is the dream of the scientific community to learn more about these planets. I just hope that we do not lose any lives in our attempts to realize this dream.

Should we be silent with regard to this lurking danger? Scientists of notable mention have pondered in silence this very question. However, this question, I am of the conviction, will be answered by the public, and not the community of scientists.

Refer to page 218 for a suggested revision of this excerpt.

Surf's up...

While you surf through cyberspace, you can learn more about pruning unneeded prepositional phrases out of your writing. One good site that discusses some of the facets of this chapter's Painless Technique is

ccc.commnet.edu/grammar/concise.htm

Practice makes permanent

We hope that studying the chapter and working the Brain Ticklers has made this first Painless Technique part of your everyday writing style. Try the following, perhaps once a week, to keep your technique sharp.

1. Using a previous writing assignment, term paper, or any other submission, examine it for preposition overuse. Pull out a paragraph or two, and use this chapter's Painless Technique to create a more concise and active excerpt.

2. Look in the editorial comment section of your newspaper and select an article written by a distinguished columnist. Notice how the writer uses simple prepositions and avoids the wordy compound prepositional phrases.

Reap your rewards

Following this technique's five-step process will make your writing clearer, more forceful, and more concise. Your readers will reward you for not making them slog through vague and wordy writing. They will reward you even more if your writing is lively and holds their interest. Sound interesting? The next chapter will explain how you can enliven your writing by using another easy-to-master technique. Let's see how it works!

CHAPTER TWO

Enliven Your Writing

DULL WORDS MEAN DULL WRITING

Have you ever picked up a story or an article that you could not put down? Try to recall what riveted you to the writing. It's likely that the action made the piece come alive. Because verbs convey action, the writer must have connected you to the writing by using lively verbs. Weak writers leave their readers unable and unwilling to identify with the page's lifeless words. If you want your writing to be something a reader cannot put down, then your next question should be

HOW DO I CONNECT READERS TO MY WRITING?

It means first getting rid of all those dull and vague verbs, and replacing them with action verbs . . . hard-hitting verbs . . . descriptive verbs.

> The boys *raced* home.
> The boys *strolled* home.
> John *glanced* at Mary.
> John *stared* at Mary.

Actions speak louder than words, unless they are action words

Is your writing lively? Rummage through some of your old writing assignments and check out the verbs that you used. Do they portray a sense of action? Do they clearly describe the characters? Just like preposition overuse, writing with dull and vague verbs is a common writing fault.

Readers will hang on your every word, but only if you provide them something interesting on which to hang. Active and descriptive verbs provide the written handholds. Writing without these types of verbs, invites readers to start skimming and possibly miss the point of your writing. Therefore, the best way to keep this situation from occurring is to eliminate those dull and vague verbs from your writing; you can accomplish this by employing the second Painless Technique. Let's take a look at it.

Painless Technique

PAINLESS TECHNIQUE No. 2: CONNECT READERS TO YOUR WRITING WITH VIVID VERBS.

IDENTIFYING THOSE HARD-WORKING VERBS

Before we can use this chapter's technique, we have to be able to identify the verbs in our writing. Since parts of speech have been pounded into your heads since grade school, you should not have any problem picking them out. Just in case, however, let's have a little review.

A verb performs one of three functions; therefore, you can identify a word as a verb if it is performing one of these three functions in the sentence. We are most familiar with verbs as the words that convey the action performed by subject. For instance,

> The student *wrote* the essay in class.
> The dog *ate* the homework.
> The cow *jumped* over the moon.

Wrote, *ate*, and *jumped* are verbs because they convey the action performed by the subject. Verbs can also express the state of the subject.

> He *loved* his family and country.
> The teacher *hoped* her best student was not absent.
> The students *believed* they were late.

Similarly, *loved, hoped,* and *believed* are verbs because they express the state or mental action of the subject. Finally, the last utility of a word functioning as a verb is to connect the subject of the sentence to a complement.

John *is* angry.

The verb *is* connects the subject of the sentence, *John,* to the complement, *angry.*

My sister *feels* sad.

The verb *feels* links the subject of the sentence, *sister,* to the complement, *sad.*

BRAIN TICKLERS
Set # 8

In the following paragraph, the author writes about a young lady named Claire. Underline the verbs and identify whether they convey Claire's physical or mental action (state) or whether they act as connecting verbs.

Claire

Claire walked down the crowded school hallway on this first day of school. She looked quickly to her left, and then to her right. Then, she walked out and joined the throng of students. Was anyone watching her? Although she wanted to look around, she kept looking straight ahead. However, it seemed that none of her classmates looked at her as they quickly walked to their classes.

(Answers are on page 219.)

Surf's up...

Need a little more practice identifying verbs? The following is a good site to surf into for some more practice:

www.gabiscott.com/bigdog/verbs.htm

After you have identified the verbs, read *Claire* again. Were you involved with the passage's events? Did the writing excerpt tell you anything about Claire, such as whether she is shy or outgoing, or whether she is pretty or plain? You cannot tell, can you? That is because the writer has not painted a vivid mental picture, so you disinterestedly sit on the sidelines. Bland writing does that to readers; consequently, bland writing penalizes student writers with lower grades and rejected submissions. You must absorb your reader into your writing's characters and action. This holds true whether you are writing a creative piece or a research paper. Let us return to the paragraph featuring Claire.

The excerpt is bland and lifeless because the verbs the writer uses to describe Claire's actions are general and impersonal. True, they denote actions, but the actions they convey are watch-from-a-distance actions. You want your reader to know what is happening, to feel a certain way about what is happening, to care about what is happening. This requires peppering your writing with vivid verbs that clearly describe the action. If you do that, you will attract and keep your reader's interest. We do that by doing the following.

Replace bland verbs with vivid verbs

Vivid verbs appeal to the reader's sense impressions and arouse feelings. Vivid verbs convey exactly what is happening and draw the reader into the action. Notice the physical and mental action verbs in the sample paragraph: *walked, saw, seemed,* and *look.* These verbs describe Claire's actions and state, but very superficially. After all, there is *walking . . .* and there is *WALKING.* There is *watching . . .* and there is *WATCHING.* General verbs such as those in our writing sample, as well as others—*go, say, come, walk, run, think, know, get,* and *tell*—usually do not explain the passage's action well enough. What is more, we want to do more than just explain; we want to *involve* the reader with the passage. *Claire* does not involve the reader because it does little to convey Claire's actions. True, we ascertain that she is moving from one point to another, as well as deduce that others are not noticing her. However, we don't know whether this is good or bad because the writer really hasn't helped us relate to Claire. An effective verb must specifically relate to its subject by personalizing the thoughts, feelings, and actions of the character. Let us change the first sentence by replacing the bland verb with a vivid verb.

Claire *swaggered* down the crowded school hallway on this first day of school.

Swaggered describes Claire's locomotion more specifically than *walked*. What do you know about Claire now? Claire has attitude. Claire wants people to notice her. Do you think she is a plain-looking girl? I doubt it. Suppose we wrote *trudging* down the hall? Would you view Claire differently? However, let us stay with the verb *swagger*, and move on to the second sentence.

She *looked* quickly to her left, and then to her right.

Although the writer realized the verb, *looked*, would have little effect on the reader, his attempt to rescue this weak, general verb by inserting a weak, general adverb, *quickly*, was unsuccessful. This is a common technique employed by writers afflicted with a bland writing style. Adverbs helping a vague verb are usually not as effective as a single strong verb in connecting the reader to the character. Ask yourself, how rapid is *quickly*? Also, think how many times you use the word *look* in your writing. This sentence demands a single vivid verb.

She *glanced* to her left, and then to her right.

Just by changing a few verbs, you can begin picturing the situation. Moving on to the next sentence:

Then, she *walked* out and *joined* the throng of students.

You should have recognized that *walk* and *join* are general verbs. We can do better; let's start by finding a vivid verb for *walk*.

Then, she *rushed* out and *joined* the throng of students.

The sentence is better, but *joined* is not doing the job for us. Let's try replacing it with a vivid verb.

Then, she *rushed* out and *merged* into the throng of students.

Moving on to the next sentence:

Was anyone *watching* her?

Again, *watching* is a general verb. To enliven this sentence, try using descriptive verbs or adverb/verb combinations such as *admiring, silently applauding,* or *appreciating.* I used *admiring,* so now we have:

Claire *swaggered* down the hall. She *glanced* to her left, and then to her right. She *rushed* out and *merged* into the throng of students. Was anyone *admiring* her?

The paragraph is beginning to come alive as we pepper it with vivid verbs. The next sentence overuses the bland verb, *look.*

Although she *wanted* to *look* around, she *kept looking* straight ahead.

Here, the author uses the weak verb, *wanted,* and the weak verb, *look,* twice. This verb selection does very little to enthuse us about what is happening to Claire. Let's try to add some life to this sentence by replacing these weak verbs with more descriptive and vivid verbs.

Although she *longed* to *notice* their admiring glances, she *stared* straight ahead.

Notice that by using the descriptive verbs, *longed* and *notice,* we have a much clearer picture of what Claire is thinking. Furthermore, note how the descriptive verb, *stared,* helps the reader better understand Claire's situation.

Good Writers Provide Their Readers Insight into the Story's Characters

Now we are getting somewhere. Let's work on the last sentence.

However, it *seemed* that none of her classmates *looked* at her as they *walked quickly* to their classes.

Again, the writer realizes the weakness of the verbs *seemed*, *looked*, and *walked*. He drops in the adverb, *quickly*, attempting to provide the reader with a little more insight. Predictably, the adverb reinforcement does not do enough. We can improve this sentence by replacing the bland *seemed* and *saw* with the descriptive verb, *ignore*. Similarly, we can pump life into the sentence by replacing the weak, *quickly walked*, with the single vivid verb, *raced*. Now we make a bold statement:

However, they *ignored* her as they *raced* to their classes.

We are finished revising the paragraph. Let us look at our new paragraph:

BETTER

Claire

Claire *swaggered* down the crowded school hallway on this first day of school. She *glanced* to her left, and then to her right. Then, she *rushed* out and *merged* into the throng of students. Was anyone *admiring* her? Although she *longed* to *notice* their admiring glances, she *stared* straight ahead. However, they *ignored* her as they *raced* to their classes.

Compare your new paragraph to the original version of *Claire*.

POOR

Claire *walked* down the crowded school hallway on this first day of school. She *looked quickly* to her left, and then to her right. She *walked* out and *joined* the throng of students. Was anyone *watching* her? Although she *wanted* to *look* around, she *kept looking* straight ahead. However, it seemed that none of her classmates *looked* at her as they *quickly walked* to their classes.

Notice how much more you know about Claire and her actions in just five sentences. We transformed the lifeless paragraph by substituting vivid verbs for general verbs or weak adverb/verb combinations:

> *swaggered* for *walked*
> *glanced* for *looked quickly*
> *rushed* for *walked*
> *merged* for *joined*
> *admiring* for *watching*
> *longed* for *wanted*
> *notice* for *look*
> *stared* for *kept looking*
> *ignored* for *looked*
> *raced* for *quickly walked*

By exchanging bland verbs for vivid verbs, we transformed mediocre writing into a paragraph that connected you to Claire. Furthermore, another benefit of substituting vivid verbs is that we reduced the wordiness of the excerpt. The original paragraph contained 65 words, whereas, the revised paragraph contains only 60 words, an 8 percent word reduction! Your teachers will thank you for enlivening your writing, as well as making it more concise.

BRAIN TICKLERS
Set # 9

Rewrite the original *Claire* by replacing at least one-half of the vague verbs with vivid verbs. However, this time, write the paragraph to portray Claire as a shy individual.

Refer to page 219 for one version of the new paragraph.

Help your readers identify with your characters

Read the following writing excerpt entitled *Joe Freeman's Spring*. Does its author provide you with a sense of how Joe feels? You get a vague idea, but it's pretty hard to identify with Joe, isn't it?

FAIR

Joe Freeman's Spring

Spring had come to western Pennsylvania unannounced. The oaks and the maples were very colorful and even the sedate elms were changing the boring line of the rundown farmhouses and barns by showing their colors. Acting as if he *owned* the town, Joe Freeman, divorced and jobless, walked down the streets of his hometown smelling the scented air of the morning. Today was a perfect day to open the door of opportunity.

Notice how by replacing the weak verbs in this following paragraph with vivid verbs, you feel more connected to Joe Freeman.

BETTER

Joe Freeman's Spring

Spring had *burst* into western Pennsylvania unannounced. The oaks and the maples were *exploding* with color and even the sedate elms were *interrupting* the boring line of the rundown farmhouses and barns by *displaying* their colors. Acting as if he *ran* the town, Joe Freeman, divorced and jobless, *strode* down the streets of his hometown *drinking in* the scented air of the morning. Today was a perfect day to *kick down* the door of opportunity.

Notice how the second paragraph used:

> *burst* instead of *come*
> *exploding* instead of *were*
> *interrupting* instead of *changing*
> *displaying* instead of *showing*
> *ran* instead of *owned*
> *strode* instead of *walked*
> *drinking in* instead of *smelling*
> *kick down* instead of *open*

The verbs in the second paragraph are not fancy verbs, but they are active verbs, and they transform a bland paragraph into interesting reading.

Strong verbs create strong feelings

Weak verbs rob your story of excitement. Notice how *The General Store* doesn't exactly leave you on the edge of your seat as you read it.

The General Store

The sun shone brightly in the sky; its hot summer heat made us tired and thirsty. We continued until we came to a small country store. We walked in and saw an old man behind the counter. He had a strange look in his eyes. Concerned, we turned around and went out the door. A cloud of dust formed behind us.

BRAIN TICKLERS
Set # 10

First, read and identify the weak verbs in the excerpt entitled *The General Store*, then rewrite the excerpt using more specific or active verbs.

Refer to page 219 for a sample rewrite.

Vivid verbs will improve all types of writing

Do not confine using vivid verbs just to creative writing assignments. Examine how the vivid verbs the author selected transformed a dull social studies paragraph into an interesting one, while conveying the same information.

POOR

Technology and capital investment are *bringing* Brazil into the next millennium. As it *changes* from socialism to capitalism, the economy is *moving* some reluctant Brazilians into the next millennium, while others are *agreeing* with the sweeping changes. The stated goal of Brazil's planners is to *control* the South American continent within five years.

BETTER

> Technology and capital investment are *propelling* Brazil into the next millennium. As it *progresses* from socialism to capitalism, the economy is *dragging* some reluctant Brazilians into the next millennium, while others are *embracing* the sweeping changes. The stated goal of Brazil's planners is to *dominate* the South American continent within five years.

Notice how the author substituted vivid verbs to illustrate the Brazilian economy.

> *propelling* instead of *bringing*
> *progresses* instead of *changes*
> *dragging* instead of *moving*
> *embracing* instead of *agreeing*
> *dominate* instead of *control*

As with *Joe Freeman's Spring*, the verbs are not elaborate, but they are forceful. We use forceful verbs when we speak, so why not use them when we write? Again, vivid verbs belong in all types of writing, and you can prove this to yourself by reading some paragraphs from publications such as *Time* and *National Geographic*. *Time* is a premier news publication, whereas *National Geographic* is the leading natural science publication. They do not fill their pages with lifeless articles. Indeed, these publications require bold, lively writing because they must interest their readers enough to read the articles. Conversely, publishing boring articles is a sure way to drive away subscribers.

What about scientific research papers? Surely, a scientific research paper has no room for vigorous verbs. That is a correct statement only if you do not want the reader to appreciate your efforts. The following excerpt illustrates how vivid verbs make scientific writing interesting. Again, the more interested the reader remains, the better chance you have of making your point.

Below is a paragraph from a report on the Moon. Notice how the author used general verbs to describe the action.

POOR

Images of the Moon *show* enormous craters across its landscape whose jagged walls *stick out* against the horizon. Millions of years' worth of debris *falling* on the satellite has *changed* its surface. However, has the landscape only been *changed* by falling debris? The flat, broad plains may be from lava *flowing* from ancient volcanoes. Volcanoes *indicate* an active subsurface, yet today, scientists *see* a quiet subsurface underneath a dead landscape. How and why was the Moon *changed*? Scientists *are looking* for the explanation to this mystery and perhaps *help* Earth from *having* the same fate.

Contrast the same paragraph, now written with vivid verbs.

GOOD

Images of the Moon *reveal* enormous craters *strewn* across its landscape whose jagged walls *jut* against the horizon. Millions of years' worth of debris *bombing* the satellite has *etched* and *pockmarked* its surface. However, has space debris *plummeting* into the surface of the Moon been the only sculptor of the landscape? The flat, broad plains *suggest* that in the early history of the Moon *surging* lava was *expelled* from ancient volcanoes. Volcanoes *demand* an active subsurface as a source of energy, yet today, scientists observe a quiet subsurface *overlain* by a dead landscape. What process *transformed* the Moon? Scientists are *striving to unlock* this mystery and perhaps *save* Earth from *suffering* the same fate.

Notice how much more interesting the second paragraph is. The information is the same as in the first passage; however, imagine slogging through a 20-page article written in the style of the first paragraph. Predictably, after a page or two, you would begin skimming the pages. Before long, you would start flipping pages, not at all interested in the information or appreciative of the hard work that went into the paper.

BRAIN TICKLERS
Set # 11

Write your own scientific, business, or technical article using vivid verbs at least half of the time.

Refer to page 220 for an example article.

SELECTING ACTION VERBS

You should now be adept at identifying weak adverb/verb combinations, which is the first step or phase of this chapter's technique. Once you have identified the offending weak verbs and adverb/verb combinations, replace at least half of them with action verbs. At first, many writers might find selecting an action verb a difficult task because they use them so infrequently they are not part of their vocabulary. Should this be a problem for you, the following table offers some vivid verbs to substitute for commonly used general verbs. Notice that the substitutes have somewhat different meanings. Nonetheless, it is this tighter fit with the sentence's subject that connects the reader. Also, refer to page 51 for a more extensive listing of vivid verbs. Use these action verbs and watch your writing come alive.

Selected General Verbs with Their Substitute Vivid Verbs

walk	talk	look	listen
stroll	chat	glance	eavesdrop
traipse	belittle	gawk	heed
ramble	debate	gaze	attend
roam	cajole	stare	detect
meander	prattle	peep	overhear

like	run	think	need
admire	scamper	meditate	covet
cherish	scramble	picture	wish
value	hustle	ruminate	desire
honor	flee	contemplate	fancy
revere	dash	imagine	crave

help	give	stop	come
encourage	impart	fetter	appear
abet	bestow	desist	emerge
support	beget	check	arise
uphold	confer	arrest	occur
back	donate	curtail	surface

tell	make	show	want
narrate	engender	exemplify	aspire
chronicle	coerce	reveal	fancy
announce	produce	divulge	yearn
urge	fabricate	proclaim	covet
deduce	erect	explain	crave

BRAIN TICKLERS
Set # 12

Use the previous list showing the possible vivid verb substitutes to rewrite the following sentences that use weak, general verbs.

1. The bank robber showed us his place for hiding the stolen money.

2. The crew made the building in less than six months.

3. I thought about joining the circus as I walked around under the big top.

4. Unaware that Marty was listening to them, Grace and Ann talked about the surprise party they were planning for him.

5. In the summertime, I eat apples by the dozen.

6. I rushed about the house as I tried to pre-pare for the party.

7. The boys spent all day looking at the cute girls.

8. The politicians spent hours talking about what was the proper course of action.

9. Jim wanted an ice cream bar all day.

10. The art exhibit showed that Picasso was the greatest artist of that era.

Refer to page 220 for some possible sentences.

Surf's up...

If you would like more ideas about dynamic verbs, check out the following site:

www.commnet.edu/grammar/progressive.htm

Do not count on adverbs to help

We have already witnessed in *Claire* that a general adverb did not portray a strong mental image. The weak adverb/verb combination is relatively ineffective compared to the vivid verb. To illustrate, let us begin with a sentence using a weak verb to describe the action of the subject.

Edgar *asked* me to lend him some money.

This sentence does little to involve or inform the reader about Edgar's actions. You can try to invite the reader to a more active role by inserting an adverb to help the weak verb.

Edgar *angrily asked* me to lend him some money.

The sentence is improving because we understand that Edgar really wants some money. However, we can improve this sentence by inserting a strong, vivid verb.

Edgar *demanded* that I lend him some money.

Compared to the original sentence, this sentence is crisp and exact because words such as *scared, happy, sad,* or *angry* rarely suffice to show the clear feelings of their holder. Moreover, converting them to adverbs by adding *-ly* does not improve matters because the vagueness remains. The way to improve any writing assignment is to demonstrate your characters' feelings and actions with specific verbs.

BRAIN TICKLERS
Set # 13

First, identify and underline the weak or vague adverb/verb combinations in *A Man's Best Friend*, and rewrite the passage by replacing at least half of the dull adverb/verb combinations that you identified with specific, vivid verbs. For help selecting vivid or descriptive verbs, use the previous table.

A Man's Best Friend

Since it was a very nice day, we decided to
slowly walk through the park. A briskly running
dog crossed our path in pursuit of a rubber
ball. He quickly took the ball in his mouth and
swiftly walked back to his owner. We could
see the dog breathing heavily as he abruptly
placed the ball at the man's feet. The man
roughly patted the dog's head.

(Answers and a sample rewrite
are on pages 220–221.)

Putting it all together

You should be able to spot weak verbs and weak adverb/
verb combinations with an eye toward substituting vivid verbs
for at least half of those offending verbs and verb combinations. Use Brain Ticklers Set # 14 to put this Painless
Technique to work.

BRAIN TICKLERS
Set # 14

Transform *Norman's Problem* by replacing
at least one-half of the general verbs and
adverb/verb combinations with active verbs.
If you need to, use the previous table to
help with this review exercise.

Norman's Problem

Norman walked into the police station and
said that he needed to talk to a police officer
immediately. The sergeant sitting at the front
desk asked that he wait his turn with the rest of
the people. The sergeant's attitude made
Norman mad. He put his hands around the
sergeant's neck and asked again to see an officer. Within seconds, several officers came, but
they came to take away Norman.

Refer to page 221 for a sample rewrite.

Practice makes permanent

You should be convinced that weak, general verbs rob your writing of action and specificity, and that, ultimately, your vague writing style will cost you in the grade book. By replacing weak
verbs and adverb/verb combinations with active, forceful verbs,
you will dramatically improve your writing. As always, honing
your new skill and making it a permanent part of your style
should be your ultimate goal. Try the following, perhaps once a
day, to keep this Painless Technique sharp.

1. Using a previous writing assignment, term paper, or any other
    submission, examine it for weak verb and weak adverb/verb

overuse. Pull out a paragraph or two, and use your newly learned technique to make the excerpt more lively and concise.

2. Select an excerpt from a front-page newspaper article. Use this chapter's technique to rewrite the excerpt. Now select an excerpt from one of the syndicated columnists in the op-ed page. Do you notice how much harder it is to find lazy verbs?

Keep your reader involved

Vivid verbs enliven your writing and keep your readers interested. Now that you know another way to liven up your writing, move on to the next chapter to learn a technique to defeat another bad writing habit that plagues many student writers.

CHAPTER THREE

Silencing the Passive Voice

THE PASSIVE VOICE ROBS
YOUR WRITING OF ENERGY

When we speak of *voice* in the context of grammar, we characterize the manner in which the verb operates in the sentence. Thus, if the sentence's subject *performs* the action or shows the condition described by the verb, we refer to the verb as an active voice verb, and we say that the writer has used the active voice. In contrast, if the sentence's subject receives the action of the verb, then we say the verb is a passive voice verb, and the writer has used the passive voice. Try to notice this distinction in the following example sentences.

ACTIVE VOICE
The pitcher threw the baseball to the catcher.

PASSIVE VOICE
The baseball was thrown by the pitcher to the catcher.

Notice with the active voice verb, the subject of the sentence, *the pitcher*, is performing the action, *throwing the baseball*. Compare this with the passive voice sentence where the action, *throwing the baseball*, is received by the sentence's subject, *the baseball*.

Where the action is

Although passive voice is useful at times, overusing it robs your writing of energy. The very structure of passive voice sentences makes them wordy and, well, passive. As we noticed, passive voice sentences relegate the subject of the sentence to receive the action rather than perform the action. Therefore, when you write in the passive voice, you de-emphasize the person, animal, or object performing the action. Consequently, even though you may not have meant to, you removed the action from your main character, which is exactly the opposite of what you want to do to keep your reader informed and enthusiastic. The effect is comparable to watching a game rather than playing it. Below are additional examples of passive voice sentences for you to read. Notice how the subject in each of the sentences (*ax, exam, application,* and *town*) is no longer the doer of the action; instead, they witness or receive the action.

> The ax was held by the woodsman.
> The exam had already been graded by the teacher.
> The application was rejected by the selection committee
>   because of the poor writing sample.
> The town has been overrun by rowdy football fans.

Stay active

Did you notice how the above passive voice sentences disconnect the real action performer from the action? Reading relies upon images, and action creates images; therefore, by transforming the unnecessary passive voice sentences into the active voice, you will

<u>TRANSFORM YOUR WRITING FROM DULL TO VIBRANT.</u>

This chapter will provide a technique for, first, identifying passive voice overuse, and then, transforming the offending sentences to the active voice.

Painless Technique

PAINLESS TECHNIQUE No. 3: CHANGE ALL UNNECESSARY PASSIVE VOICE SENTENCES TO ACTIVE VOICE SENTENCES.

RECOGNIZING AND CHANGING THE PASSIVE VOICE

Passive voice overuse is one of the most common culprits of weak writing. Fortunately, this writing fault is easy to correct, and doing so pays large dividends from your teachers; however, to use the Third Painless Technique to improve your writing, you must first be able to recognize a passive voice sentence. Once you have identified a sentence written in the passive voice, you must transform the offending passive sentence into an active voice sentence. To begin, let us learn how to quickly spot passive voice writing.

Identifying the voices

In the active voice, the subject of the sentence always performs the action or exists in a condition described by the verb. Also, in active voice sentences where there is a direct object, the direct object receives the action performed by the subject. Below are examples of sentences written in the active voice. Notice how the action stays connected to the performer of the action in the following examples of sentences written in the active voice. This subject-verb connection gives your writing life and keeps the reader interested.

ACTIVE VOICE SENTENCES

The band (subject) *played* well.

Matt (subject) *kicked* the ball (direct object) into the goal.

Katie (subject) *served* the volleyball (direct object) over the net.

The teacher (subject) *had been gone* all week.

Subjects in passive voice sentences do not perform the action described by the verb; rather, these subjects receive the action. The doer of the action is now either stuck in a prepositional phrase or left out of the sentence completely.

PASSIVE VOICE SENTENCES

The ball *was kicked* into the goal by Matt (subject).

The volleyball *was served* over the net by Katie (subject).

The class *had been cancelled*.

(In the above sentence, the writer implies the prepositional phrase, *by the teacher*, containing the subject, *teacher*.)

After looking at the above sentences, you should now know that you have spotted a passive voice sentence whenever the verb describes the action *performed on* or *done to* the subject. Stated differently,

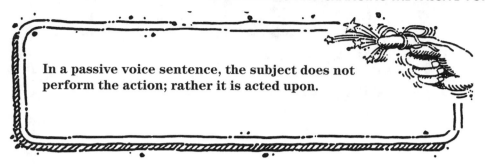

In a passive voice sentence, the subject does not perform the action; rather it is acted upon.

Furthermore, passive voice sentences are always built with some form of *to be* + the past participle of a verb that acts upon the subject (either stated or implied) of the sentence. The following are some additional examples of passive voice sentences.

> Arthur *was selected* by Ms. Jones to be the class representative.
> Arthur *was selected* to be the class representative.
> The house *had been painted* by the work crew.
> The house *had been painted*.
> The gold medal *was won* by the figure skater.
> The gold medal *was won*.

Notice that the doers of the action in each sentence (*Ms. Jones, the work crew, the figure skater*) have lost their center spotlight in these passive voice sentences. You should now realize that passive sentences disconnect the performer and the action, and the result is dull and stilted reading.

Surf's up...

If you want a little more help identifying the active voice and passive voice before tackling the Brain Tickler, surf over to these sites:

www.gabiscott.com/bigdog/active_passive.htm
people.whitman.edu/~hasimry/passive.htm

BRAIN TICKLERS
Set # 15

Determine the voice of each of the sentences below.

1. The dog barked all day.

2. The dog ran after the fire truck.

3. The firemen were reprimanded by the mayor.

4. The championship trophy was won by the Cardinals.

5. The girls sang loudly.

6. The sisters had argued over the car for an entire week.

7. John had been away for a long time.

8. New York was selected by the committee as the site for its annual meeting.

9. The saxophone player received an encore.

10. The secretary is answering the telephone.

11. The football field was wet.

12. All occurrences of the passive voice were eliminated by the student writers.

13. The violinist practiced every day.

14. The writing teacher was not pleased with the essays.

15. John stayed after class to meet with the teacher.

16. Bob had stopped at every traffic light.

17. The compositions were returned by the teacher at the end of class.

(Answers are on pages 221–223.)

Three steps change your voice

Now that we can identify passive voice sentences, let us learn the following three-step procedure for converting them to active voice sentences. By learning this simple procedure, we will be ready to apply this chapter's Painless Technique of changing all unnecessary passive voice sentences to active voice sentences.

Step One:

Identify a passive verb sentence by looking for a verb form that consists of *both* the past participle and a form of *to be* that acts upon the subject.

For instance, look at the following sentence:

Norma Jean *was selected* by the seventh grade to present their demands.

The verb, *was selected*, acts upon the sentence's subject, *Norma Jean*. Therefore, this sentence is written in the passive voice.

Once you have identified a passive voice sentence such as the one above, you are ready for Step Two.

Step Two:

Locate the person or thing in the sentence performing the action. This noun will be either part of a prepositional phrase or absent from the sentence (but implied by the writer).

In our sentence, *the seventh grade* performs the action.

Step Three:

Convert the action-performing noun or the noun whose condition is displayed into the subject of your revised sentence. Usually, the subject of the original sentence becomes the object in the active voice sentence.

Applying the three-step technique to the original sentence yields the revised sentence; notice how the original subject, *Norma Jean*, is now the direct object.

The seventh grade selected Norma Jean to present their demands.

Notice that the revised version contains over 15 percent fewer words than the passive voice sentence, which demonstrates that active voice sentences are not only livelier, but they are more concise.

BRAIN TICKLERS
Set # 16

Use Painless Technique No. 3's three-step process to transform the passive voice sentences of Set # 15 to active voice sentences.

(Answers are on pages 223–225.)

WHEN THE PASSIVE VOICE IS NECESSARY

Your writing will immediately improve because you are now an expert at identifying passive voice writing and transforming it to the active voice. However, there are times, and they are rare, when the passive voice is preferred. The following are the special situations requiring the passive voice.

Special passive situation no. 1

The passive voice is necessary whenever you do not know, or do not want to clearly reveal, the action performer. The following sentences demonstrate this situation.

Thunderstorms and hail *had been forecast* for the morning of the field trip.

In this passive voice sentence, the writer has chosen not to reveal that *meteorologists* had forecast the thunderstorms.

Noises *were being made* all over the house.

Here, *scurrying mice* could have made the noises. However, the writer chose not to reveal this to the reader.

The swimming meet *has been postponed.*

The writer chose not to reveal that the meet director had postponed the swimming meet.

The day *has been ruined.*

The day may have been ruined *by thunderstorms*; only the writer knows.

BRAIN TICKLERS
Set # 17

Determine whether the following sentences are written in the active or passive voice. If the sentence is written in the passive voice, determine whether it should remain in the passive voice because the writer does not know or does not want to clearly reveal the source of the action.

1. Threats were being issued throughout the tense ordeal.

2. The summit meeting had been convened.

3. The student council meeting was convened by Bob.

4. His fate had been foretold.

5. His fate had been foretold by the fortune-teller.

6. The military secrets had been stolen.

7. The spy stole the military secrets.

8. The military secrets had been stolen by the spy.

9. Trash was being thrown all over the yard.

10. John threw trash all over the yard.

(Answers are on pages 225–226.)

Special passive situation no. 2

Passive voice verbs are also necessary when the person or thing receiving action is more important than the one performing the action.

The Queen of England was welcomed by all.
The class field trip was postponed.
The Kentucky Derby had been run by hundreds of horses.

In the example passive voice sentences, the *Queen of England*, the *class field trip*, and the *Kentucky Derby* are more important as receivers of the action than the performers of the action. Therefore, the passive voice is necessary to show their relative importance.

BRAIN TICKLERS
Set # 18

Determine which of the following sentences should remain in the passive voice because the writer feels the person or thing receiving the action is more important than the person or thing performing the act.

1. The football game had been lost by the team.

2. The queen was sighted by her loyal subjects.

3. The hurricane was sighted by the terrified residents.

4. The Super Bowl will be broadcast by Channel 2 in one week.

5. The president will be interviewed by the newscaster.

(Answers are on pages 226–227.)

Special passive situation no. 3

If a sentence contains two verbs with the same subject, a shift of voice, either from active to passive, or passive to active, may be necessary to preserve the flow of the sentence.

> The Tigers *won* the championship game, and *were awarded* the Governor's Trophy.

The verbs shift from the active (*won*) to passive (*were awarded*); however, they have the same subject, *the Tigers*. Since both the verbs have the same subject, using the passive voice helps the flow of the sentence. Compare this sentence to one where using both voices creates confusion and wordiness.

> As *we gazed* at the horizon, *the sailboats were seen* against the setting sun.

Notice, the subject of the active voice verb (*gazed*) is *we*. However, switching to the passive voice (*was seen*) caused the author to shift the subject (*sailboats*). The shift from the active to the passive voice (or vice versa) in the above sentence leaves the sentence confusing and stilted because the writer shifted subjects as well. In so doing, the action flow was disrupted. Avoid changing voices if doing so causes you to change subjects as well. Notice that the above sentence can be more clearly written in the active voice.

> As *we* gazed at the horizon, *we* saw the sailboats against the setting sun.

Surf's up...

Want more information on when to use the passive voice?

Check the following site:

ccc.commnet.edu/grammar/passive.htm

BRAIN TICKLERS
Set # 19

Determine which of the following sentences should remain unchanged although they contain both passive voice and active voice verbs.

1. The band finished rehearsal and was given a well-deserved rest.

2. As the king surveyed his empire, treachery was plotted by his enemies.

3. Before the campers left, the wolves had been heard howling in the woods.

4. The campers ventured into the woods and were attacked by wolves.

5. The wolves ran away as the hunters were heard calling for help.

(Answers are on pages 227–228.)

PUTTING IT ALL TOGETHER

To reiterate, situations where writing in the passive voice is necessary occur relatively infrequently. Once you determine that your writing does not require one of the above three situations, use the three-step process to reduce the unnecessary passive voice sentences in your writing submission.

BRAIN TICKLERS
Set # 20

Apply this chapter's Painless Technique to improve the following writing excerpt, *Anna at the Science Fair*. Use the technique's three-step process to transform the unnecessary passive voice sentences to active voice sentences. Keep in mind the special situations that require the passive voice. The number in parentheses at the end of the paragraph is the word count of the excerpt. You should also notice how your new paragraph is more concise, as well as easier to comprehend.

Anna at the Science Fair

Anna worked all summer on her Science Fair presentation and was rewarded for her hard work. She was selected by her school to represent it at the district Science Fair. Her science teacher was surprised by her experiment's innovation. At the Science Fair, Anna's findings were applauded by the judges as insightful. Later that day, her presentation was awarded the grand prize by the impressed judges. As she received her award, her proud parents could be seen taking photographs. The Science Fair had been a tremendous success! (87)

Refer to page 228 for a suggested rewrite.

WHAT ABOUT WRITING A SCIENTIFIC PAPER?

Good science is gathering results from objective studies and objectively reporting them. Unfortunately, some teachers mistake objectivity of results with the illusion of objectivity created by writing in the third person. Their logic is simple, but flawed. They correctly observe that the active voice will necessarily require an increased use of the first person—*I observed this*, or *We performed the following tests*. Unfortunately, *I* and *we* are mistakenly viewed as too subjective, and this rationale leaves the third person as the objective writer's only alternative. This mistaken notion encourages writing in the passive voice: *The following tests were performed* . . .

The following excerpt illustrates the unfortunate result associated with writing a scientific paper in the disassociated, passive voice style.

POOR

Saturn

Observations were made by the scientists from the University of California regarding the rings of Saturn. It is the analysis and conclusion of this group that ice, frozen gasses, and rock particles comprise the rings of Saturn. Further observations will be made by the group as an understanding of the relationship between the rings of Saturn and the moons of Saturn is the goal of the group. (67)

Imagine reading several pages of that style of writing! It is difficult to imagine much excitement directed toward their findings. In contrast, pick up any *Scientific American* magazine and read the feature articles. You will notice very little passive voice writing in them because the magazine editors and the writers want the readers to read the articles. Therefore, they communicate with their readers in a concise and direct way without sacrificing objectivity. You should do the same when you are writing a scientific paper. Do not confuse objective with detached and wordy.

BRAIN TICKLERS
Set # 21

Rewrite the wordy, passive voice excerpt entitled *Saturn* so that it is concise and active. Notice how you can keep the scientific nature of the paragraph, and yet make it interesting. The number in parentheses represents the word count of the excerpt. Notice how much you have reduced the word count by rewriting the unnecessary passive voice sentences in the excerpt.

(Sample rewrite is on page 228.)

Practice makes permanent

You should be convinced that the passive voice is the enemy of a concise and interesting writing style. By learning the Painless Technique for spotting passive voice writing, and changing it to improved active voice writing, you are well on your way to dramatically improving your writing. As always, honing your new skill and making it a permanent part of your style should be your ultimate goal. Try the following, perhaps once a day, to keep this technique sharp.

1. Using a previous writing assignment, examine it for passive voice overuse. Pull out a paragraph or two, and use your newly learned technique to make the excerpt more concise and active.

2. Select a magazine article from a national magazine such as *Sports Illustrated* or *Time*. Try to spot passive voice use. Notice how few instances you find. Get the idea?

Activate your reader for a favorable reaction

This chapter's technique will reward your reader with more interesting and concise submissions, and you with better grades. Now that we have conquered the passive voice, let us examine another writing style that will rob a submission of life—overusing nominalizations.

CHAPTER FOUR

Reduce Nominalizations and Activate Your Writing

NOMINALIZATIONS EXPOSED!

You should realize by now that you cannot impress your readers unless you keep them interested in the words on the page. Writing in a boring, stuffy style is a sure way to lose your reader's interest, and without their interest there is no possibility of earning a better grade. One writing flaw that creates an extreme case of boring, stuffy writing is overusing nominalizations. Since we want to improve our writing, the first question we have to ask is: What is a nominalization?

A *nominalization* is a noun derived from a verb or an adjective. Examples of a noun deriving from a base verb include *seclusion, inference,* and *confinement.* You can spot these verb-based nouns by their suffixes: *-ent, -ence, -ant, -ency, -ancy, -ment, -tion,* and *-sion.* Similarly, adjective-based nouns derive from a base adjective. Adding the suffixes *-ent, -ant, -ful, -able* converts adjectives into nominalizations. Below are some common nominalizations created from verb and adjective bases.

Verb	Nominalization	Adjective	Nominalization
move	movement	thoughtful	thoughtfulness
excited	excitement	difficult	difficulty
withdraw	withdrawal	opulent	opulence
fail	failure	applicable	applicability
accept	acceptance	elastic	elasticity

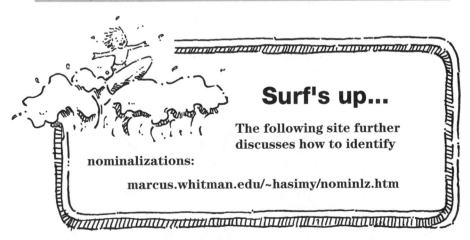

Surf's up...

The following site further discusses how to identify nominalizations:

marcus.whitman.edu/~hasimy/nominlz.htm

Unfortunately, many students burden their writing with nominalizations because they mistakenly believe this writing style is sophisticated. However, rather than leading to polished writing, overusing nominalizations creates vague, stilted writing. Whereas,

REDUCING NOMINALIZATIONS LIVENS UP YOUR WRITING.

Verbs create action, not nouns

Why does overusing nominalizations create vague and stilted writing? The answer lies in the nature of nouns. A *noun* refers to a person, place, quality, idea, or thing. By its very nature, any noun or noun form cannot convey motion or action to the reader, nor can it describe itself. As we learned in Chapter Two, crisp and interesting writing demands well-placed verbs and adjectives.

Why not just add some verbs and adjectives to the nominalizations to return action and description to the writing? Unfortunately, it is not that easy because whenever you begin inserting verbs and adjectives, wordiness, the other culprit of bad writing shows up. There are two ways to attach nouns to sentences; the first way is with verbs, and the second way is with prepositions. The writer overusing nominalizations, therefore, must find verbs or prepositions to connect the nominalizations to the sentence. Moreover, nominalizations' word structures and their typical place in the sentence promote the use of weak, vague verbs and accompanying adverbs to buttress the weak verb. Chapter Two demonstrated the consequences of trying to help weak verbs with adverbs: more words, but no more action. Notice how we can write the sentences avoiding nominalizations and how the rewritten sentences are more active and concise. The numbers in parentheses denote the number of words in the sentence.

POOR
Bob made a *withdrawal* of money from his bank account. (10)

BETTER
Bob *withdrew* money from his bank account. (7)

POOR
You can make *application* of these techniques to your writing. (10)

BETTER
You can *apply* these techniques to your writing. (8)

POOR
The rubber band has a lot of *elasticity*. (8)

BETTER
The rubber band is very *elastic*. (6)

You can avoid stuffy writing by applying this chapter's Painless Technique. Let's take a look at it.

Painless Technique

PAINLESS TECHNIQUE NO. 4: IDENTIFY, THEN TRANSFORM UNNECESSARY NOMINALIZATIONS INTO FORCEFUL VERBS OR DESCRIPTIVE ADJECTIVES.

Identifying nominalizations

The first part of this chapter's Painless Technique requires that you identify the offending nominalizations. If you need to, review the first part of this chapter to help become comfortable identifying nominalizations. Once you are ready, try the following exercises that test your ability to identify nominalizations in your writing.

BRAIN TICKLERS
Set # 22

Identify and underline the nominalization in each of the following sentences, then determine the verb or adjective root along with the suffix used in creating that nominalization. The numbers in parentheses denote the number of words in the sentence.

1. The senator had no recollection of his campaign promise. (9)

2. The teacher's reaction to the news was a negative one. (10)

3. Each candidate is under investigation before his nomination. (8)

4. Many political prisoners have not had the benefit of representation by counsel. (12)

5. The discussion of the class was on the field trip. (10)

6. The mayor's office started an investigation into the council member's actions. (11)

7. The husband and wife made a renewal of their wedding vows. (11)

8. The newspapers launched an attack of a vicious nature at the candidate. (12)

9. The induction of the baseball player into the Hall of Fame took place on Friday. (15)

10. Katie's reaction was predictable. (4)

11. Matthew made the suggestion that we stop at the campsite. (10)

12. The editorial is a reflection of the writer's thoughts. (9)

13. Bob's writing improvement astounded everyone. (5)

14. The carelessness of his writing was apparent throughout the entire manuscript. (11)

15. The general signaled for a withdrawal of his troops. (9)

16. By your acceptance of this check, you agree to paint the house. (12)

(Answers are on pages 228–230.)

Baggage, baggage, and more baggage

If you are not yet convinced that using too many nominalizations ruins
your writing, consider the following: Not only does overusing nominalizations drain the life out of your
writing, but this bad writing habit
adds a lot of unnecessary words
that waste your readers' time. The
bulk of the wordy baggage comes
from prepositional phrases that
result whenever you convert verbs
and adjectives into nouns that
become the objects of the prepositional phrases. Examine the sentences below that contain
nominalizations.

The boys, full _of excitement_, entered the room

The sentence contains the nominalization, _excitement_,
which also carries with it the prepositional phrase baggage,
of excitement.

The _departure_ of the students created a chaotic scene.

This sentence contains the nominalization, _departure_, which
requires an accompanying wordy prepositional phrase, of the
students, to convey the writer's thoughts.
As you can see, by writing the sentences with a nominalization, the writer needed to add a prepositional phrase. Recall the
Chapter One discussion of how using too many prepositional
phrases weakens your writing.

More words, less action

You should now see that dullness and wordiness result when
writers overuse nominalizations. Do the following exercise to
make sure you can spot both of these problems resulting from
this bad writing habit.

BRAIN TICKLERS
Set # 23

Read the following paragraph entitled *The English Teacher*. Notice that although the paragraph is wordy, it contains relatively few verbs and many nominalizations. Identify the nominalizations that plague this passage.

The English Teacher

The English teacher had little expectation that her class would attain improvement in their writing. There are few indications that her opinion of the situation should be under reconsideration. However, a discussion among the students yielded a different conclusion because they were unwilling to make an acceptance of her conclusion. It was their decision to have a discussion with the principal about the replacement of their teacher. They realized, nevertheless, that the principal would have a reluctance to accept their suggestion.

(Answers are on page 230.)

WRITING SITUATIONS THAT CREATE UNNECESSARY NOMINALIZATIONS

The second part of this chapter's Painless Technique requires you to eliminate the unnecessary nominalizations that you have identified in your writing submission so that your writing will be more lively and concise. Eliminating unnecessary nominalizations is a rather easy task in that it requires only that you reverse the process that you used to create them. In other words, you must convert the nominalization to its verb or adjective root. The key to this technique is being able to identify the writing situation where this nominalization overuse usually occurs. The good news is that the overuse usually confines itself to four situations in which the weak writer typically inserts a nominalization where a verb or adjective would have been a better choice. Below are those situations where writers mistakenly use nominalizations along with the remedies for converting the misused nominalizations to their adjective or verb roots.

Situation no. 1: nominalization trails a weak verb

The most common writing error involving nominalizations occurs whenever the writer inserts a nominalization after a vague verb. This situation occurs because the vague verb didn't convey the action of the sentence well enough so the writer mistakenly tries to help out with a noun. Now, instead of one writing problem (the vague verb), the writer adds the unnecessary nominalization attempting to help out the vague verb. The result is a dull and wordy sentence. Observe the following sentences depicting nominalizations trailing a weak verb.

POOR
The commander has no *expectation* that the prisoners will be freed.

BETTER
The commander does not *expect* that the prisoners will be freed.

POOR
The candidates have made a *withdrawal* of their offers to debate on the issues.

BETTER
The candidates *withdrew* their offers to debate on the issues.

Notice that the nominalizations in each of the sentences (*expectation* and *withdrawal*) follow dull and general verbs within those sentences (*has* and *has made*). To improve the first sentence, replace the nominalization, *expectation*, with its root verb, *expect*. In the improved second sentence, the verb, *withdrew*, replaces the nominalization, *withdrawal*, and substitutes for the original weak verb, *have made*.

Situation no. 2: nominalization inserted after an expletive

The next situation occurs where writers include a nominalization in an expletive construction. An expletive construction is a sentence that begins with such words as *there are, there is*, or *it is*. Because expletive constructions sometimes cause the reader to lose track of the subject, the writer drops in a nominalization to help refer the reader to the subject in the sentence. However, doing so only makes the original confusing sentence confusing *and* dull. Changing the nominalization to a verb, and then finding a subject for the verb can easily correct this nominalization misuse situation.

POOR
There is no need for *acceptance* of this condition.

BETTER
You do not need to *accept* this condition.

POOR
There are *indications* that he is quitting.

BETTER
He *indicated* that he is quitting.

POOR
There has been no *movement* of the weak foundation.

BETTER
The weak foundation has not *moved*.

POOR
It is Matt's decision to play the soprano saxophone in the jazz band.

BETTER

Matt *decided* to play the soprano saxophone in the jazz band.

Notice how the rewritten sentences convey more of a sense of action and are more concise.

Situation no. 3: nominalization is the subject of a weak verb

Using vague verbs creates yet another nominalization overuse situation, but this time the writer uses a nominalization as the subject of the empty verb. The problem here is that the nominalization actually forms from a stronger verb than the verb the writer has chosen. The way to remedy this bad writing situation is to change the nominalization to its root verb and then create a new subject for the sentence.

POOR

The *decision* of the teacher is to re-grade the test.

The nominalization, *decision*, is the subject of the weak verb, *is*. Also, notice that the writer must include the prepositional phrase, *of the teacher*, to complete the sentence.

BETTER

The teacher *decided* to re-grade the test.

POOR

Our *discussion* concerned the test.

Here, the nominalization, *discussion*, takes on the role of subject for the weak verb, *concerned*.

BETTER

We *discussed* the test.

Situation no. 4: consecutive nominalizations

The final nominalization overuse situation is where the writer uses consecutive nominalizations because the writer correctly realizes that one nominalization is weak and ineffective, but then mistakenly tries to remedy the situation by adding yet another nominalization. Notice the weak verbs in the sentences containing nominalizations.

The remedy is to take advantage of the root verbs of these nominalizations. As mentioned earlier, they are more active and descriptive than the filler verbs the writer has used to connect the nominalizations. Once you change one or both nominalizations to verbs, you must then create subjects for those verbs.

POOR

The general is involved in a *discussion* of the *movement* of the troops.

Here we have the option to convert one or both of the nominalizations to their root verbs. To complete the sentence, we selected *general* as the new subject.

BETTER

The general *discussed* the movement of the troops.

or

The general *discussed* where the troops had *moved*.

POOR

The *withdrawal* of the troops was under *consideration* by the president.

In this situation, we can fix the original sentence by now using *president* as the subject and converting one or both nominalizations to their root verbs.

BETTER

The president *considered* the withdrawal of the troops.

or

The president *considered* whether to *withdraw* the troops.

BRAIN TICKLERS
Set # 24

The following sentences suffer from nominalization overuse. Identify which of the four situations each sentence represents.

1. The admiration of the teacher by the class was apparent.

2. Our consideration of the matter is that it is unimportant.

3. Recognition and acceptance of a problem is the first step toward solving it.

4. Our solution to the problem is important to us.

5. The boys have no remembrance of their misdeed.

6. There is recognition of the player's effort.

7. The coach has come to the conclusion that his efforts are in vain.

8. There has been no indication by the strikers that they are giving in.

(Answers are on pages 230–231.)

APPLYING THE TECHNIQUE

Now that you are skilled at identifying nominalizations, it is time to apply the second part of the Painless Technique and transform them into forceful verbs or descriptive adjectives.

POOR

Reorganizing Congress

Our Congress should begin *reorganization*. Predictably, there is *opposition* to this idea by most of the members of Congress. However, I believe this *movement* would gain the *favor* of the voters. Moreover, my first *inclination* would be to favor a *reduction* in the size of both legislative bodies because adequate *representation* could be accomplished with fewer elected officials. Unfortunately, the *reaction* of the lawmakers has been in *opposition* to this *suggestion*. They have given us the *indication* that their position is in our best interests. However, their *opposition* is selfish, and is not a *reflection* of critical *thought*. (98)

The 98-word excerpt contained 14 nominalizations. Furthermore, the writer used only 11 verb sets, and most were of the form *to be*, which is a weak verb. Moreover, the passage contained far too many prepositional phrases. Let us see how to improve submissions like *Reorganizing Congress*. We begin with the first sentence:

Our Congress should begin *reorganization*.

This sentence illustrates Situation No. 1: A nominalization (*reorganization*) following a weak verb (*begin*). To improve this sentence, change the nominalization to its root verb, which can replace the empty verb. Our new sentence reads:

Our Congress should *reorganize*.

Let's examine the next sentence:

Predictably, there is *opposition* to this idea by most of the members of Congress.

This sentence is Situation No. 2: Nominalization inserted after an expletive. This sentence can be improved by converting the nominalization, which is *opposition*, to its root verb, *oppose*, and then specifically stating a subject to link to this more forceful verb. For our subject, let's use *most members of Congress*. Therefore, our improved sentence reads:

Predictably, most members of Congress *oppose* this idea.

Sentence No. 3:

However, I believe this *movement* would gain the *favor* of the voters.

This sentence is similar to Situation No. 4, which illustrates consecutive nominalizations. (Note: The nominalization form and verb forms of *favor* are identical.)
To improve this sentence, change one or both nominalizations to the root verb forms and find a subject for each verb. Let us use the verb *favor* and the subject *voters* in the new sentence.

However, the voters would *favor* this movement.

Sentence No. 4:

Moreover, my first *inclination* would be to favor a *reduction* in the size of both legislative bodies because adequate *representation* could be accomplished with fewer elected officials.

Again, this is Situation No. 4: Consecutive nominalizations. This situation requires changing one or both nominalizations and then finding a subject for each verb. Choosing to transform both nominalizations, we create

> Moreover, I would be *inclined* toward *reducing* the size of both legislative bodies because Congress could adequately *represent* us with fewer elected officials.

Sentence No. 5:

> Unfortunately, the *reaction* of the lawmakers has been in *opposition* to this *suggestion*.

This is another Situation No. 4 sentence, although now we have three nominalizations: *reaction, opposition,* and *suggestion*. Applying this chapter's technique entails changing one or all of the nominalizations to verbs and then creating a subject for each verb.

> Unfortunately, the lawmakers' reaction is to *oppose* this *suggestion*.

Our next sentence is:

> They have given us the *indication* that their position is in our best interests.

This sentence depicts Situation No. 1 because the nominalization *indication* trails the weak verb, *have given*. We can improve this sentence by first transforming the nominalization to its root verb, *indicate*, and then replacing the original weak verb, *have given*, with the root verb. We write our new sentence:

> They *indicate* that their position is in our best interests.

The final sentence:

> However, their *opposition* is selfish, and is not a *reflection* of critical thought.

This is another Situation No. 4 sentence. Again, the technique requires us to change one or both of the nominalizations to verbs and then create a subject for each verb.

However, their *opposition* does not *reflect* any critical thought.

Now let us look at the nominalization-reduced paragraph:

BETTER

Reorganizing Congress

Our Congress should reorganize. Predictably, most members of Congress oppose this idea. However, the voters would favor this movement. Moreover, I would be inclined toward reducing the size of both legislative bodies because Congress could adequately represent us with fewer elected officials. Unfortunately, the lawmakers' reaction is to oppose this suggestion. They indicate that their position is in our best interests. However, their opposition does not reflect any critical thought. (70)

Not only is the excerpt clearer, it is less wordy. The rewritten excerpt contains 70 words, whereas the original nominalization-ridden excerpt contained 98 words. Using the chapter's technique, not only have we made the paragraph more active, we have reduced the wordiness by more than 20 percent!

Surf's up...

Everyone is avoiding nominalizations, even in cyberspace.

Check out this site:

www.gened.arizona.edu/gonzalez/writing.htm

Now it is your turn to transform nominalization-plagued sentences into concise, vibrant sentences.

BRAIN TICKLERS
Set # 25

Convert the sentences in Set # 22 containing
nominalizations into sentences that are lively
and concise. Check the number in parentheses
at the end of each sentence in Set # 22; this is
the number of words in the sentence. Compare
the number of words in your revised sentence
to the original sentence.

Refer to pages 231–232 for
suggested revised sentences.

NECESSARY NOMINALIZATION SITUATIONS

In some limited cases, nominalizations are useful, even necessary. Let us examine those limited situations that require nominalizations.

Situation no. 1: the nominalization is a subject referring to a previous sentence

John was late for school and lost his English notebook. His chronic *carelessness* brought about these predicaments.

Notice how the above nominalization *carelessness* helps link the second sentence to the first sentence.

Katie practiced playing her French horn every day. This *dedication* helped her become an accomplished horn player.

Again, the nominalization, *dedication*, links the second sentence to the first.

Another instance in which nominalizations are necessary occurs where they represent concepts that are difficult to explain with only a few words.

Situation no. 2: nominalizations referring to well-known concepts

The debate focused on the Flag Burning *Amendment*.

Rather than state that the debate focused on the revision or addition proposed to the Constitution of the United States, the writer simply uses the nominalization, *amendment*.

Freedom of expression is certainly a charged topic open to debate.

Again, rather than write about the exemption from arbitrary restriction by civil authorities, the writer simply writes the nominalization, *freedom*.

As you can see, there are times when it is easier to describe familiar concepts rather than make your reader slog through a clause full of nouns and verbs. Concepts such as *death, love,* and *hate* are others that can be best expressed as nominalizations. Notice, however, that these are relatively narrow situations, much like the passive voice exception of the last chapter. After you have determined that the encountered nominalization does not fall into one of these situations, eliminate it using this chapter's technique.

BRAIN TICKLERS
Set # 26

The following paragraph is plagued with nominalizations. Transform the excerpt into a concise and interesting piece by reducing the nominalizations, where appropriate. Also, take note of the reduced word count.

Writing Well

It is my contention that writing well is a matter of learning a few simple techniques. Ignorance of these techniques will no longer be a matter of acceptance by teachers. Therefore, there is no need for your acceptance of poor writing skills. Nonetheless, I know that your inclination is toward disagreement. However, I do not make this statement without the offer of proof. Take my suggestion, and try these techniques for one month. If after one month, you see no improvement, then seek help. (84)

Refer to page 232 for a revised paragraph.

Practice makes permanent

Overusing nominalizations is detrimental, no matter what type of piece you are writing. As with all the other Painless Techniques, honing your new skill and making it a permanent part of your style should be your ultimate goal. Regularly, try the following to keep your technique sharp and part of your permanent writing style.

1. Using a previous writing assignment, examine it for nominalization overuse. Pull out a paragraph or two, and use your newly learned technique to make the excerpt more understandable and concise.

2. Select an excerpt from an exciting book you have read or are reading. First, notice the lack of nominalizations, and then rewrite a paragraph or two using some nominalizations and notice how they affect the clarity and flow of the writing.

Keep it flowing

This chapter's Painless Technique, as well as the previous chapters' Painless Techniques that you have mastered, will put you on the road to good writing. We can make it even more enjoyable by smoothing out the writing road. The next chapter shows how to make your writing flow across the pages.

CHAPTER FIVE

Smoothing Out Your Writing

CONFRONTING CHOPPY WRITING

Has the word *choppy* ever been written on one of your papers? If so, your teacher was trying to tell you that your writing was stopping and starting with each new sentence, rather than smoothly flowing throughout. Poor transitions between sentences and between paragraphs are one of the main causes of choppy writing. Let us examine some choppy writing examples and see if we can spot what is causing the problem. Let's start with a passage entitled *Ms. Mahoney*.

Ms. Mahoney

Ms. Mahoney is an English teacher in my school. She is convinced that her students have been shortchanged. Ms. Mahoney spoke with the principal about developing a writing program. She had a program already worked out. The principal rejected her idea. The program had been set for the school year. She told her she would consider her request next year. Ms. Mahoney knows that will be too late for her students.

What makes *Ms. Mahoney* rather unpleasant to read? Read it again, but this time read it aloud. Notice how you paused at the end of each sentence and began at the start of a new sentence. Did you notice how frequently you started and stopped? That is because this paragraph is nothing more than a series of short, direct statements, and when strung together, they create a choppy piece of writing. Because this paragraph does not flow well, it is difficult for you to follow the writer's thoughts. Imagine reading page after page written in this style!

The table below sets forth the number of words and the sentence type in *Ms. Mahoney*. Let's take a look at the table and see if it can help us.

Ms. Mahoney *Sentence Analysis*

Sentence	Number of Words	Type
1	9	Declarative
2	9	Declarative
3	11	Declarative
4	7	Declarative
5	5	Declarative
6	9	Declarative
7	10	Declarative
8	11	Declarative

The *Ms. Mahoney* excerpt typifies choppy writing. Consequently, we can assume that whatever makes this excerpt choppy probably causes a choppy style in other writing. Our sentence analysis table helps us locate the cause. Observe that every sentence is a declarative sentence that contains 11 words or less. This means that you should watch for strings of short declarative sentences that will cause your reader to stop and start too frequently. Let's examine another sign of this poor writing style.

Read the following writing passage. Better yet, just as you did with *Ms. Mahoney*, read *Improving Writing Skills* aloud. Can you determine why it does not flow well?

Improving Writing Skills

It is my belief that the writing skills of any student can be improved. There is enough evidence in the form of compositions handed in before and after English courses. There are some students who benefit more than others from writing instruction. This is because they apply themselves.

It is a problem that can be easily corrected. There are programs that teachers, like myself, have created that can be immediately implemented. It is unfortunate, however, that there are teachers who are opposed to any methods that have not been previously used. It is of no consequence to them that "the way we have always done it" methods are ineffective.

Again, let's examine the passage one sentence at a time using a sentence structure table to help us spot any patterns.

Improving Writing Skills *Sentence Analysis*

Sentence	Words	Type	Introductory Words
1	14	Declarative	It is
2	16	Declarative	There is
3	12	Declarative	There are
4	6	Declarative	This is
5	9	Declarative	It is
6	14	Declarative	There are
7	20	Declarative	It is
8	18	Declarative	It is

Once again, the excerpt reads in a stop-and-start manner; we observe that although the sentences are all declarative, they contain a significant number of words. Therefore, we don't seem to have the string of short declarative sentences problem. So what is the problem? Refer to the last column, *Introductory Words*. This column displays the words that begin each sentence. Notice the pattern?

The pattern is that every sentence begins with an expletive construction. We ran across expletive constructions in Chapter Four when we discussed the negative impact on your writing caused by overusing nominalizations. Well, they are back, this time in the context of choppy writing. You will recall that a sentence beginning with the words *it* or *there* (*expletives*, in this instance) are followed by a form of the verb *be*, and the subject of the sentence is referred to as an *expletive construction*. Expletive constructions usually begin as follows:

> There is . . .
> It is . . .
> There are . . .

Read through the passage *Improving Writing Skills* below. The expletives and their accompanying *be* verbs have been italicized. Notice how they prevent the sentences from flowing into one another, resulting in a piece of choppy writing.

Improving Writing Skills

It is my belief that the writing skills of any student can be improved. *There is* enough evidence in the form of compositions handed in before and after English courses. *There are* some students who benefit more than others from writing instruction. *This is* because they apply themselves.

It is a problem that can easily be corrected. *There are* programs that teachers, like myself, have created that can be immediately implemented. *It is* unfortunate, however, that there are teachers who are opposed to any methods that have not been previously used. *It is* of no consequence to them that "the way we have always done it" methods are ineffective.

Now, study a recent sample of your writing. If paragraph after paragraph contains several of these constructions, be aware that your sentences are weakly connected. By beginning nearly every sentence with an expletive, you set up your writing to be nothing more than a series of unconnected declarative sentences.

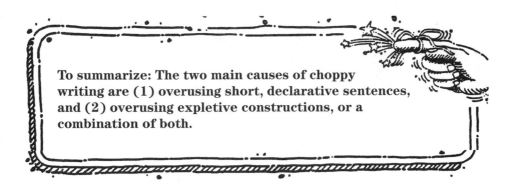

To summarize: The two main causes of choppy writing are (1) overusing short, declarative sentences, and (2) overusing expletive constructions, or a combination of both.

What you usually discover whenever you talk to students who have just written a choppy piece is that they have written something different, at least in their mind; they connected the sentences in their mind, but not on paper. That is why it is so important to spot the signs of choppy writing, because merely reading over your writing may not always help you catch your writing flaw.

This next exercise will help you make sure that you can spot the signs of choppy writing.

BRAIN TICKLERS
Set # 27

Good Writing Skills is an example of choppy writing. Identify the sentence structure that causes the stilted style.

Good Writing Skills

Good writing skills must be learned. Writing skills are like any other skill. It is well known that poor writers have improved their writing. There are many examples at both the middle school and high school level. There are some students who improve more than others. There is hope for everyone, however.

It is easy for students to improve their writing. I am one of those who improved. There are still times when I write poorly but they are not as numerous as before. It is as a result of better writing that my grades have improved.

(Answers are on pages 232–233.)

Now that you can spot the signs of choppy writing, you are ready to learn the Painless Technique for smoothing it out.

Painless Technique

PAINLESS TECHNIQUE NO. 5: USE CONNECTING WORDS, PHRASES, AND PUNCTUATION TO SMOOTHLY LINK YOUR WRITING.

SMOOTH YOUR WRITING BY LINKING YOUR SENTENCES

This chapter's technique employs three methods to ensure that your sentences relate to each other.

Sentence linking method no. 1: use linking words to connect sentences

The first method proposes that we use linking words. The concept underlying the first method is that each sentence should leave a "hook" for the sentence preceding it and the sentence following it. These hooks connect the consecutive sentences together in one of the following ways:

1. By *comparing* facts or concepts in the consecutive sentences.

2. By making the sentences *reinforce* one another.

3. By making the consecutive sentences demonstrate a *consequence* of an action.

4. By allowing consecutive sentences to state information that follows in logical *continuity*.

If you use effective transitions, your sentences will relate to one another by comparison, reinforcement, consequence, or continuity. Certain words facilitate this linking. Some of these linking words are shown below by their functional category.

Comparison	Reinforcement	Consequence	Continuity
similarly	for instance	as a result	next
although	in addition	consequently	after
instead	for example	therefore	finally
nevertheless	moreover	thus	secondly
but	also	nevertheless	and

Examine the paragraph about Ms. Mahoney on page 103. Notice how the absence of linking words made it difficult to read. We can improve the paragraph's flow by combining the short sentences to form complex ones, and then using linking words to hook the revised sentences. Let's see how we can improve *Ms. Mahoney*, beginning with the first two sentences:

> Ms. Mahoney is an English teacher in my school. She is convinced that her students have been shortchanged.

These two short declarative sentences can be combined into a longer sentence that will provide information that connects it to the next sentence.

> Ms. Mahoney, an English teacher in my school, is convinced that her students have been shortchanged in the development of their writing skills.

In the next sentence, we notice that it contains no connecting hook to the previous writing.

> Ms. Mahoney spoke with the principal about developing a writing program.

We can link this sentence to the first part of the paragraph by showing the *continuity* of Ms. Mahoney's actions.

> At the *beginning* of the school year, Ms. Mahoney spoke with the principal about developing a writing program for the students.

The next three sentences are weakly linked. Unfortunately, the writer probably envisioned their connection in his or her mind, but was unable to set it down on the paper.

> She had a program already worked out. The principal rejected her idea. The program had been set for the school year.

We can use *consequence* and *comparison* to hook the sentences to one another, as well as to the previous sentences.

> *Although* she had a program already worked out, the principal rejected her idea *because* the program had been set for the school year.

The next sentence is another short declarative sentence standing alone.

> She told her she would consider her request next year.

We can use *comparison* to link it to the previous sentence.

> *Instead*, she told her that maybe the school would consider her request next year.

The last sentence does little to complete the paragraph because it relates poorly to the preceding sentences.

> Ms. Mahoney knows that will be too late for her students.

We can use *consequence* to hook this sentence to the preceding sentences and provide a conclusion for the paragraph.

> *Nonetheless*, Ms. Mahoney knows that it will be too late for her students.

Now compare the revised passage to the original one, and notice how much better the sentences flow and how much more enjoyable it is to read.

Ms. Mahoney

Ms. Mahoney, an English teacher in my school, is convinced that her students have been shortchanged in the development of their writing skills. At the beginning of the school year, Ms. Mahoney spoke with the principal about developing a writing program for the students. Although, she had a program already worked out, the principal rejected her idea because the program had been set for the school year. Instead, she told her that maybe the school would consider her request next year. Nonetheless, Ms. Mahoney knows that it will be too late for her students.

Surf's up...

The next time you are out surfing, check out the following site that discusses transitions between sentences:

www.csun.edu/hflrc006/transit.html

You have seen how words that create hooks between sentences improve the flow of a writing piece, and now it is your turn to try our Painless Technique's first method.

BRAIN TICKLERS
Set # 28

Use the first method of this chapter's Painless Technique—for smoothing out choppy writing—to rewrite the following paragraph. Your goal should be to create hooks that smoothly link the sentences.

Summertime

Our family enjoys summer vacation. We usually go on a long trip. My aunt lives in New Orleans. We often travel to see her. Sometimes she comes to our house. We go on a trip together. We went to the Grand Canyon last year. We really enjoyed ourselves.

See page 233 for a possible revision.

In your revised paragraph, notice how you successfully used linking words to enable the shorter sentences to work together, making it easier for the reader to envision a sequence of events.

Let us examine another of the Painless Technique's methods for smoothing choppy writing.

Sentence linking method no. 2: use demonstrative pronouns and relative pronouns to link sentences

A *demonstrative pronoun* is a pronoun that refers to a specific, person, place, or thing; we can use this reference to connect sentences. Examples of demonstrative pronouns are

- *This*
- *That*
- *These*
- *Those*

Read the following piece of choppy writing and then notice how demonstrative pronouns can help the flow of the paragraph.

POOR

Away from Home

John could not wait to leave home and go off to college. He told his parents every day. He looked at going away to college as going on a vacation. He would come to find out he was incredibly wrong. He spent every night in the library studying until midnight. He recalled what he had said to his parents. This was his first semester at college.

The paragraph makes sense, but lacks continuity. Let's see how we can improve it. Notice below how demonstrative pronouns join the disconnected sentences and help make the passage flow. Let's look at the first two sentences:

> John could not wait to leave home and go off to college. He told his parents every day.

The writer has related the two short declarative sentences, but not connected them. We can link the two sentences with a demonstrative pronoun.

> John could not wait to leave home and go off to college, and he told his parents *this* every day.

The demonstrative pronoun, *this*, connects the contents of the second sentence to the contents of the first sentence. Look at the next two sentences:

> He looked at going away to college as going on a vacation. He would come to find out he was incredibly wrong.

Again, these two relatively short declarative sentences do not connect. However, we can turn to demonstrative pronouns for help.

> He looked at going away to college as going on a vacation. *That* idea, he would come to find out, was incredibly wrong.

Notice how we can relate the second sentence back to the first one by beginning the second sentence with *that idea*. Proceeding to the next two sentences:

> He spent every night in the library studying until midnight. He recalled what he had said to his parents.

Here again we are confronted by short declarative sentences that do not connect. However, we can utilize demonstrative pronouns to join the sentences together.

> Every night *that* he was in the library studying until midnight, he recalled *those* words he had said to his parents.

We are now at the last sentence:

> This was his first semester at college.

Notice how this short declarative sentence neither links to the preceding sentences, nor does a good job of wrapping up the paragraph. We can remedy both shortcomings with a demonstrative pronoun.

Such was his first semester at college.

Now, as you compare the rewritten passage to the original one, notice how the demonstrative pronouns help your reading flow from one sentence to the next.

BETTER

Away from Home

John could not wait to leave home and go off to college, and he told his parents this every day. He looked at going away to college as going on a vacation. That idea, he would come to find out, was incredibly wrong. Every night that he was in the library studying until midnight, he recalled those words he had said to his parents. Such was his first semester at college.

Demonstrative pronouns provide you with another way to combat choppy writing, and with a little practice, you will have no trouble using this method.

BRAIN TICKLERS
Set # 29

Use demonstrative pronouns to connect the sentences in *The Mascot*.

The Mascot

Our high school does not have a mascot. Many of the students were upset because the school was without a mascot. The students decided to run a contest to see who could select the best mascot. The contest turned into a disaster. The students wanted a cute mascot. A cute mascot would show how friendly our school was. A cute mascot was unacceptable to the basketball players. The basketball players wanted the mascot to be ferocious looking. The principal had to end the contest. We still do not have a mascot.

Refer to page 233 for a possible revision.

USING RELATIVE PRONOUNS

You have seen how demonstrative pronouns linked several disconnected sentences; relative pronouns can perform the same service. You may recall that a *relative pronoun* refers to a person, place, or thing that preceded it. Examples of relative pronouns are

- *Who*
- *Which*
- *Where*
- *That*

This referencing function serves to link the present and preceding sentence. Notice how relative pronouns link the ideas and facts of the successive sentences in this excerpt. First, read the version of *Country Living* without the relative pronoun connectors.

POOR

Country Living

I love the serenity of the country. It is the place that recharges me. I can be myself there. My closest neighbors are the Bradfords. They live over a mile away. They are wonderful people. I cannot think of anywhere else that I could live so well.

117

Next, read the excerpt where the writer has taken advantage of relative pronouns.

BETTER

> ## *Country Living*
>
> I love the serenity of the country. It is the place that recharges me, and one *where* I can be myself. My closest neighbors, the Bradfords, *who* live over a mile away, are wonderful people. *Where* else could one live so well?

Now it is your turn to use relative pronouns to fix a piece of choppy writing.

BRAIN TICKLERS
Set # 30

The Modest Coach is another piece of choppy writing. Employ the most recently discussed method of using relative pronouns to connect the sentences so that the excerpt flows.

The Modest Coach

I was surprised when the team won all of its games. I do not know if anyone was expecting the team to win every game. Warren Peese gave the credit to the players. He has been the coach of the school for 15 years and has always avoided praising himself. Most coaches would not have missed the opportunity to take at least some credit.

Refer to page 233 for a possible version.

USING SEMICOLONS

Relative and demonstrative pronouns create smooth transitions between sentences. Let us investigate the last of this technique's methods to make your writing flow smoothly. This method involves linking certain sentences with a semicolon.

Sentence linking method no. 3: use a semicolon to link closely related statements

Many writers avoid using semicolons because they are not sure when they are appropriate. The next chapter discusses their use in more detail, but for now, it is enough to say that the semicolon acts to link two closely related facts or concepts, or more precisely, two independent clauses. Notice how the semicolon helps join the ideas contained in short sentences. In the example below, a semicolon helps hook the short declarative sentences together.

POOR
Maria quit her job. She thought about it a lot. She knew she made the right decision.

BETTER
Maria quit her job; she thought about it a lot and knew she made the right decision.

Notice how the semicolon links Maria's actions in the first sentence with her thought process revealed by the two short sentences that followed. Let's review another example where the semicolon helps connect short, disjointed sentences.

POOR

Matt is the best speaker in the school. He is the leader on the speech and debate team.

Again, we are confronted with short declarative sentences. Therefore, we can use a semicolon to combine the short sentences into one sentence that is easier to read.

BETTER

Matt is the best speaker in the school; he is the leader on the speech and debate team.

TRANSITIONING PARAGRAPHS

We have seen how it is important to connect sentences within the paragraph, but it is also important to connect the paragraphs within the submission. Disconnected paragraphs lead to the same choppy writing caused by disconnected sentences. Just as it lacks smoothly flowing sentence-to-sentence transitions, many students' writing lacks smooth transitions between paragraphs. Let us examine how we can correct that writing flaw.

Surf's up...

Here is another great site for more help on linking sentences:

forms.flashbase.com/forms/transitions.htm

We link paragraphs together for the same reason that we link sentences to one another. The following three methods can be employed to connect your paragraphs, and thereby create a smooth flow to your writing submission.

Paragraph linking method no. 1: introductory linking words and phrases

The first method suggests opening each paragraph with a linking word or phrase. Let's see how this works by first looking at an excerpt where the writer failed to link the paragraphs.

POOR

One expert on military affairs determined that we are in a more perilous situation now with the collapse of the Soviet Union than we have ever been. He argues that the so-called "peace dividend" is wishful thinking by Americans. Terrorism and growing third world military powers have replaced the controlled might of the Soviet Union.

The United States must be more on its guard, not only outside of its borders, but inside as well. Expenditures for military and security forces will increase rather than decrease, as many politicians are fond of telling their constituents. This means even less available money for social problems than during the Cold War days.

Americans are truly much safer from the threat of a world war than they have been in the last 100 years, and that is good news for all of us.

Notice how the writing sample below connects the paragraphs with a linking word or a linking phrase.

BETTER

One expert on military affairs determined that we are in a more perilous situation now with the collapse of the Soviet Union than we have ever been. He argues that the so-called "peace dividend" is wishful thinking by Americans. Terrorism and growing third world military powers have replaced the controlled might of the Soviet Union.

Thus, the United States will have to be more on its guard, not only outside of its borders, but inside as well. Expenditures for military and security forces will increase rather than decrease, as many politicians are fond of telling their constituents. This means even less available money for social problems than during the Cold War days.

Nevertheless, in spite of this gloomy news, Americans are truly much safer from the threat of a world war than they have been in the last 100 years, and that is good news for all of us.

Paragraph linking method no. 2: repeating key words

The second method for linking paragraphs involves using a key word at the end of one paragraph, and then repeating it at the beginning of the next paragraph. Notice below how the key word *interest* links the facts of the first paragraph to the hoped-for consequence set forth in the second paragraph. First, however, let's look at the disconnected excerpt.

POOR

The candidates engaged one another in a series of debates throughout the state. The debates were lightly attended, but were viewed by many voters on television. The candidates were surprised by the voters' interest. Apathy toward statewide elections was common in the past.

The candidates are hoping for a 50 percent voter turnout, rather than the usual 20 percent.

BETTER

The candidates engaged one another in a series of debates throughout the state. The debates were lightly attended, but were viewed by many voters on television. The candidates were surprised by the voters' *interest*. Apathy toward statewide elections was common in the past.

The candidates are hoping this *interest* in the debates carries over into the voting booths on election day. They are hoping for a 50 percent voter turnout, rather than the usual 20 percent.

Paragraph linking method no. 3: ask and then answer a question

The last method involves finishing one paragraph with a question, then answering the question in the following paragraph. Notice in the revised excerpt how the second paragraph links the first and third paragraph by answering the first paragraph's question and posing a question for the third paragraph to address.

First, the disconnected paragraph:

POOR

Teachers from all over the United States are attending the national conference. The conference is noted for encouraging dialogue concerning difficult issues facing the teachers. The conference agenda is packed with discussion items. One receiving the most attention deals with programs and techniques for helping students to write better.

Writing is a skill activity, and like all skill activities, repetition is the key to success. We encourage athletes and musicians to practice and hone their skills. We should do the same with student writing.

Many argue that writing differs from sports and music because athletes and musicians require only muscle repetition to attain proficiency, whereas writing proficiency requires applying certain techniques to abstract thoughts.

BETTER

Teachers from all over the United States are attending the national conference. The conference is noted for encouraging dialogue concerning difficult issues facing the teachers. The conference agenda is packed with discussion items, but the one receiving the most attention deals with the question: *"How can we help our students write better?"*

In spite of the complexity of the question, *the answer may be as simple as, "Just make them write more."* Writing is a skill activity, and like all skill activities, repetition is the key to success. We encourage athletes and musicians to practice and hone their skills; *why not take the same road with student writing?*

Educators respond to this suggestion differently. Many argue that writing differs from sports and music because athletes and musicians require only muscle repetition to attain proficiency, whereas writing proficiency requires applying certain techniques to abstract thoughts.

When confronted with composing a piece with several pages of paragraphs, the above three methods should be used in variety so as not to make the piece sound trite by using predictable paragraph transitions. Use the following exercise to incorporate these paragraph-connecting methods into your writing.

BRAIN TICKLERS
Set # 31

Use the Painless Technique's methods to link the sentences within the paragraphs, as well as linking the paragraphs of *Stress in Our Contemporary World*.

Stress in Our Contemporary World

Eating and exercise habits affect a person's health. Heredity plays a part in determining a person's longevity too. Some scientists believe stress affects a person's health. They are trying to determine why people are under more stress today than they were a generation ago. They are also trying to find a way to alleviate that stress. I feel that stress grows as civilization progresses. Other researchers do not embrace my view.

There are more people in the world today than there ever have been. This is one cause for the increasing level of stress. Information moves faster than it ever has. There is also more of it. Civilization cannot progress without people and information.

The interaction of people and information will be important in the future. Studies show that we can be overloaded with information. This makes people anxious, and even violent. We should seek solutions to these problems.

Refer to pages 233–234 for one possible revision.

Practice makes permanent

At this point, you should realize that choppy writing is the enemy of an interesting writing style. By learning this Painless Technique's methods for smoothing out your writing, you are well on your way to dramatically improving your writing style. As always, honing your new skill and making it a permanent part of your style should be your ultimate goal. Try the following, perhaps once a day, to keep this technique sharp.

1. Examine a previous writing assignment for choppy writing. Pull out a paragraph or two, and use the Painless Technique's methods to help the writing flow.

2. Select three or four nonconsecutive paragraphs from a magazine article. Using linking words, phrases, and sentences, try to create a smooth transition between the paragraphs.

KEEP YOUR WRITING FLOWING

With a little practice, your writing should flow across the pages. This chapter's techniques and the techniques that you have learned in other chapters will greatly improve your writing style—but we are not yet through. Many bad writing habits, such as passive voice writing and using too many short declarative statements are often rooted in a writer's inability to punctuate the longer compound and complex sentences. Why is this?

One answer is that students who are uncomfortable with their ability to punctuate these sentences will often write short, choppy sentences. The problem emanates from their lack of skill using the simple comma to punctuate the more complex sentences. If you are one of these students, the next chapter demonstrates a technique that shows you how to use the comma to transform short, choppy sentences into longer, flowing ones.

CHAPTER SIX

Harness the Power of the Comma

POLISHING YOUR WRITING WITH COMMAS

Do short sentences dominate your writing? You may recall one of your English teachers telling you that a <u>simple sentence</u> consists of a single *independent clause* and no *dependent clauses*. Unfortunately, that definition does not tell us much unless we understand independent and dependent clauses. So, let's take a look at them.

A <u>dependent clause</u> is a clause containing a subject and a verb; however, it does not express a complete thought. Therefore, a dependent clause cannot constitute a complete sentence and must be paired with one or more independent clauses to create a sentence. Within the sentence, a dependent clause is introduced either by subordinate conjunctions, such as *since, because, if,* or *when,* or relative pronouns, such as *which, who,* or *that.* The dependent clauses are italicized in the sentences below.

> *Since the students had done so well on the test,* the teacher gave them the day off.
> *If you enjoy writing,* you should enroll in Dr. Novo's English class.
> Our band, *which meets every Wednesday after school,* will perform in the school auditorium next week.
> Jenny, *who is our class president,* is always trying to make her friends aware of important social issues.

In contrast, an <u>independent clause</u> is a clause that contains a subject and a predicate that can stand alone as a complete sentence.

Since the students had done so well on the test, *the teacher gave them the day off.*

If you enjoy writing, *you should take Dr. Novo's English class.*

Our band, which meets every Wednesday after school, *will perform in the school auditorium next week.*

Jenny, who was our class president, *was always trying to make her friends aware of important social issues.*

As you see, an independent clause is a simple sentence, and because simple sentences consist of only one independent clause, most simple sentences are brief. Below are some examples of typical simple sentences.

The teacher entered the classroom.
The car ran off the road.
The student finished the writing assignment.

Filling your writing with simple sentences, such as those in the example, may create a choppy piece of writing. However, this chapter's Painless Technique will help you to avoid this unfortunate result.

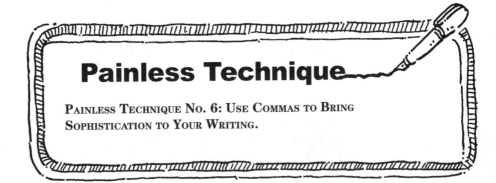

Painless Technique

PAINLESS TECHNIQUE No. 6: USE COMMAS TO BRING SOPHISTICATION TO YOUR WRITING.

You will see how the comma helps create long flowing sentences because it enables you to address several ideas in one sentence. In this chapter we discuss a few simple methods for spotting situations where using the comma will not only make your writing flow, but also better present your ideas.

GROWING BEYOND
THE SIMPLE SENTENCE

One way to improve your writing is to progress from a simple style to a sophisticated style. Consequently, we want to move beyond that plain style with its simple sentences, and we can do that, in part, just by using the simple but powerful *comma*.

The sentences that we are striving to write to break up the monotony of choppy sentences fall into three categories.

Compound sentences

The first category is the *compound sentence*. A compound sentence contains two or more independent clauses, but no dependent clauses. Notice in the following examples of compound sentences how a comma and a coordinating conjunction join the independent clauses.

> I went to John's house, but he was not home.
> The student studied all night, yet he failed the test.
> The band performed on Tuesday, but their Wednesday performance was canceled.

Compound sentences constitute the first step toward moving beyond simple sentences. By moving from the simple to compound sentence, we can compare or link events and ideas that were confined to separate sentences. Moreover, because compound sentences are usually longer sentences, we can use them to help make the passage read more smoothly. Next, let's look at the next category of more elaborate sentences, the complex sentence.

Complex sentences

A *complex sentence* is a sentence that includes one independent clause and one or more dependent clauses. Notice how the comma separates the dependent clause (single underline) from the independent clause (double underline).

> Because clear-cut forests hold less water, the vegetation suffers.
> Since she enjoyed writing, Katie kept a journal.
> If you enjoy writing, you should try to read books suggested by your teacher.

Complex sentences provide us with an even greater framework within which to express multiple ideas, and like compound sentences, including them in your writing enables the passage to flow more smoothly. Moving on to the most sophisticated of the sentences, the compound-complex sentence, we can see how the comma helps to create this type of sentence.

Compound-complex sentences

The *compound-complex sentence* is a sentence containing two or more independent clauses and at least one dependent clause. Notice how the comma separates the dependent clause (single underline) from the independent clauses (double underline).

> While Matt was sleeping, his parents decorated the house for his birthday and his sister baked him a cake.
> At the mayor's request, the city council adjourned and the city controller resigned.

Surf's up...

If you want to know more about sophisticated sentences, the following web site discusses their structures:

uottowa.ca/academic/arts/writcent/
hypergrammar/sntstrct.html

THREE METHODS FOR CREATING SOPHISTICATED SENTENCES

Our goal is to use commas to combine two or more simple sentences into a flowing compound, complex, or compound-complex sentence. With that goal in mind, this chapter's Pain-less Technique provides three methods for using the comma to upgrade your writing.

Method no. 1: use a comma with an introductory phrase

A stubby declarative sentence often can be transformed to an introductory phrase, then combined with another short sentence or sentences to form a flowing sentence. The first method suggests that you use the comma to create an introductory phrase. In so doing, you create a dependent clause that can be used to write a complex or compound-complex sentence. Let us examine phrases that work particularly well as introductory phrases by beginning with the participial phrase.

The Participial Phrase

A *participial phrase* begins with a participle, which is merely the verb form of a word, ending in *-ing* (present participle) or *-ed* (past participle) that is derived from a verb. The phrase includes additional words that together with the participle function as an adjective. The following are some examples of present and past participial phrases.

PRESENT PARTICIPIAL PHRASES

Disappearing into the crowd, the thief eluded the police.

Scavenging for an easy meal, the gulls help to keep the beach clean.

PAST PARTICIPIAL PHRASES

Scared to ring the doorbell, the children stood frozen at the door.

Elated with her test scores, Jennifer applied to Harvard and Stanford.

The following examples demonstrate the method of converting a declarative sentence to a participial phrase, and then combining the phrase with another sentence to create a more sophisticated sentence.

POOR

John was bored with life. He set out to see the world. The first leg of his trip was going to take him to Mexico City. (26)

Let's work on those first two unexciting sentences. Notice that by rewriting the first sentence into a participial phrase, *bored with life*, and using it as an introductory phrase for the subsequent sentence, we can transform the passage.

BETTER

Bored with life, John set out to travel the world. The first leg of his trip was going to take him to Mexico City. (24)

Another benefit of this method is that it cuts down on wordiness because it eliminates common words in both of the short sentences. For instance, in the above example, we eliminated the pronoun reference to the subject, *John*, in the second sentence (*he*), as well as the weak verb, *was*, in the first sentence.

Below is another example illustrating a situation in which we can employ the participial phrase as an introductory phrase.

POOR

Marty has studied grammar. Therefore, she felt more comfortable in her writing.

Transform the above sentences by changing the first sentence into the participial phrase, *having studied grammar*, an introductory phrase to create the subsequent complex sentence.

BETTER

Having studied grammar, Marty felt more comfortable in her writing.

Again, notice the decreased number of words in the revised sentence. Not only is the passage more flowing, but it is less wordy. Let's look at one last example of converting a simple sentence into a participial phrase and then using this phrase to introduce the second sentence. As before, the result is a more elaborate sentence.

POOR

Margaret was excited by her progress. She moved on to the next lesson.

Converting the first sentence into a participial phrase, *excited by her progress*, and then using it to introduce the subsequent sentence can improve the above passage. Notice the word count of both passages.

BETTER

Excited by her progress, Margaret moved on to the next lesson.

Surf's up...

The following web site provides examples of the power of the comma in improving your writing:

info2.harper.cc.il/writ_ctl/comma9.htm

Watch out!

Beware of the dangling participle! Notice that in all of the above examples the participial phrase refers to the subject of the sentence. Let's take a look at an example.

Having studied grammar,
Marty felt more comfort-
able in her writing.

The participial phrase,
having studied grammar,
refers to the subject of the
sentence, *Marty*. The sentence
makes sense when this relationship between the participial
phrase and the subject remains
intact. Let's look for this relationship in another example.

Excited by her progress,
Margaret moved on to
the next lesson.

Likewise, the participial phrase, *excited by her progress,*
refers to the subject of the sentence, *Margaret*. The sentence
makes it clear that Margaret is progressing because she is en-
couraged by her progress. However, let's examine what
happens when the writer incorrectly modifies the subject with a
participial phrase.

Having recently died, I thought of Jim every day.

How can you think of
someone when you are
dead? Obviously, the writer
meant that the subject, *I*,
thought of the recently
deceased, *Jim*, every day.
Unfortunately, the writer
modified *I* rather than *Jim*
with the participial phrase.

The above examples
showed you how a par-
ticipial phrase's value can
help make your writing flow. Now try the following exercise to
see if you can use participial phrases to convert short simple
sentences to a flowing sentence.

BRAIN TICKLERS
Set # 32

For each pair of sentences, convert one sentence to a participial phrase so that it acts as an introductory phrase for the second sentence. When you are finished, the two simple sentences should be combined into one flowing sentence. Also, take note of the word count in your revised sentence.

1. Joe was angered by Tim. He slammed down the telephone. (10)

2. Mary is very embarrassed to participate in class. She answered a question for the first time yesterday. (17)

3. The students were excited about learning at the beginning of the term. They were bored by the end of the term (21).

4. Jason was very excited at the thought of receiving presents. He stayed up all night. He was the first one in the living room on Christmas Day. (27)

5. When we leave depends upon the weather. We will leave tomorrow if the weather is close to being pleasant. (19)

6. The baby is sitting in his high chair. He is ready to eat. (13)

7. The hermit was removed from society. He had little use for contemporary technological advances. (14)

8.   The young jockey had just won the
     Kentucky Derby. She now set her sights on
     the prestigious Preakness. (18)

(Answers are on page 234.)

You have seen how the participial phrase and the comma can
help make your writing flow. Now look at another type of phrase
that, together with the comma, can help mature your writing.

The Prepositional Phrase

Another way to create an introductory phrase is to convert a
simple sentence to a prepositional phrase and then set the
phrase off with a comma so that it forms an introductory clause
for a complex or compound-complex sentence. We have already
learned about *prepositional phrases*, which are phrases that
begin with a preposition and include the preposition's object
and its modifiers. Below are some examples of prepositional
phrases.

> *With the flow,*
> *Under the oak tree,*
> *Against all odds,*

Many times, a prepositional phrase can transform a boring
little sentence into a phrase that will introduce a complex sentence. Consequently, the two simple sentences can form a complex or compound-complex sentence. Let's look at an example
with two simple sentences.

POOR
The eighth-graders performed the opening act. The characters
were angry at each other.

Converting the first sentence into a prepositional phrase, *in
the opening act performed by the eighth-graders*, and then
using it as an introductory phrase for the subsequent
sentence can transform the above sentence into a complex
sentence.

BETTER

In the opening act performed by the eighth-graders, the charac-ters were angry at each other.

Again, we see how two simple sentences can be transformed into a flowing complex sentence by creating a prepositional phrase set off by a comma.

POOR

The moon glowed overhead. The boys enjoyed the stillness of the night.

Converting the first sentence into a prepositional phrase, *with the moon glowing overhead,* and then using a comma to set it off from the second sentence, we can write a mature complex sentence.

BETTER

With the moon glowing overhead, the boys enjoyed the stillness of the night.

Prepositional phrases play the same important role as participial phrases. Together, these two types of phrases in conjunction with the comma help to make your writing flow and comprise the first method of this chapter's Painless Technique. Before we move on to the next two methods associated with our Painless Technique, try working through the following exercise to make sure you can use prepositional phrases.

BRAIN TICKLERS
Set # 33

For each pair of sentences below, convert one sentence to a prepositional phrase that can be used as an introductory phrase for a complex sentence.

1. The team played their hearts out in the first game. They continued to play that way throughout the season.

2. I won first place in the writing competition. I worked hard.

3. Buying the boat was against his better judgment. He bought the sailboat.

4. The antagonist and protagonist opened the play. They were engaged in a very long dialogue scene.

5. The parents waved good-bye to their son. He raced off to enjoy his newfound freedom as a college student.

6. Mr. Jones voted for the current mayor. He might have voted for the challenger if the circumstances were different.

7. Sarah's English teacher accompanied her. They left for the meeting with the principal at two o'clock.

(Answers are on page 235.)

Together, the introductory clause and the comma are powerful tools that you can use to smooth out choppy writing. Let's examine another method that can also improve writing plagued by numerous simple sentences.

Method no. 2: use a comma and a coordinating conjunction to link simple sentences

The second method of this chapter's Painless Technique uses the comma and a coordinating conjunction to join two independent clauses (simple sentences) to create a flowing sentence. Recall that an *independent clause* is a group of words containing a subject and verb, and expresses a complete thought. We will see that commas and coordinating conjunctions must work together, and therefore, commas can link independent clauses only if they have the help of a coordinating conjunction. The usual coordinating conjunctions are *and, but, or, nor, so, for,* and *yet.* Let's see how this method works by looking at the following examples where two independent clauses create a choppy writing segment.

POOR
The students respect Ms. Martin. Similarly, she respects her class.

The choppy clauses form a longer, smoother sentence after being linked with a comma and the coordinating conjunction, *and.* Now we have

BETTER
The students respect Ms. Martin, *and* she respects her class.

Let's try the method again on the following bit of choppy writing.

POOR
Ms. Martin wanted to be a writer. Her fondness for children convinced her to teach.

Here, the independent clauses or simple sentences can form a longer sentence by connecting them with a comma and the coordinating conjunction, *but*

BETTER

Ms. Martin wanted to be a writer, *but* her fondness for children convinced her to teach.

It is important to remember that this method requires *both* the comma and the coordinating conjunction to join two or more independent clauses, and that omitting the coordinating conjunction creates a writing error known as the *comma splice.* The following example illustrates this common writing error.

POOR

The composition is terribly worded, only a complete rewrite will help it.

This is a typical attempt by the author to combine two short sentences into a longer sentence by using a comma; however, a comma splice results, thus making the sentence difficult to understand. In this example, a coordinating conjunction such as *and* is needed.

BETTER

The composition is terribly worded, *and* only a complete rewrite will help it.

Again, we begin with the choppy writing

POOR

I decided to improve my writing. I just didn't know how.

A writer trying to combine the sentences with only a comma falls victim to the comma splice.

WORSE

I decided to improve my writing, I just didn't know how.

This chapter's method requires *both* a comma and a coordinating conjunction. The choppy writing can be smoothed as follows:

BETTER

I decided to improve my writing, *but* I just didn't know how.

Surf's up...

Comma splices in cyberspace!
This site also shows you how to
avoid the dreaded comma splice:

www.chumpchump.com/csfs.13.c.ex.htm

BRAIN TICKLERS
Set # 34

Use the chapter's Painless Technique for using commas to combat choppy writing to combine the following simple sentences into a flowing sentence.

1. Mr. Martin is concerned about our writing skills. He did not change his teaching style.

2. I want to listen to the music. I can't because the baby is sleeping.

3. We went out to eat. Then, we went to a movie.

4. The team put up a valiant fight. They lost in the fourth quarter.

5. Bob and Helen decided to eat at the new restaurant. They invited Ann.

6. We were angry at all the traffic. We called the mayor's office.

7. Jason felt that both candidates were qualified. He chose not to vote on Election Day.

8. Mary wanted to live in Boston. She has never lived in the Northeast. She has never been away from home.

Refer to pages 235–236 for some possible sentences.

Method no. 3: let the comma and semicolon join forces

Choppy writing can also result from repeated phrases. Many writers, by repeating certain parts of sentences to provide the reader with facts or opinions, end up with a series of choppy, repetitious sentences. The comma can be helpful in this instance, also. The third method of this chapter's technique frees your writing from repetitious wording by suggesting using a semicolon to link the repetitious short sentences and a comma to replace the repeating words. The following example shows the technique's method for eliminating choppy, repetitious sentences.

POOR

John elected to attend Stanford. Mary elected to attend Harvard.

Combine the choppy sentences into a single sentence without losing any information.

BETTER

John elected to attend Stanford; Mary, Harvard.

Notice how the repetitious words, *elected to attend*, in the second sentence could be eliminated. To make sure that you can use the Painless Technique's last method to improve your writing, work through the following exercise.

BRAIN TICKLERS
Set # 35

Use this chapter's final method of using the comma in tandem with the semicolon to combat choppy writing in the following sentences.

1. I am taking English this semester. My sister is taking pre-algebra this semester.

2. My brother lives in Alaska. I live in Hawaii.

3. Cassandra earned an A on her essay. John earned a B on his essay. Marsha earned a B on her essay.

4. We are traveling to Iceland this spring. We will be going to Bermuda this winter.

(Answers are on page 236.)

This chapter's Painless Technique illustrates using the comma to smooth out your writing. To review, the Painless Technique consists of three methods where, in certain situations, commas can

1. Create introductory phrases

2. Combine independent clauses

3. Eliminate repetition

Surf's up...

Glide into these sites for more information about using the

powerful comma:

www.aci-plus.com/tips11.htm
commnet.edu/grammar/commas.htm
**uottowa.ca/academic/arts/writcent/hypergrammar/
comma.html**

We learned how each method smoothes the stilted writing into flowing prose. To test your understanding of this chapter's Painless Technique, do the following exercise.

BRAIN TICKLERS
Set # 36

Apply the rules of this chapter's technique to *Rachel's Dream*. Remember that your goal is to create a smoothly flowing paragraph.

Rachel's Dream

Rachel had never given much thought about what she was going to do when she grew up. She has now decided to become a writer. Creativity runs in her family. Her brother is a writer. Her sister is a screenwriter. Mr. Stones is her English teacher. He told her that she had a talent for writing. She responded by starting a writing journal. Now she is writing in it every day. Rachel is excited about writing a best-seller. She knows that she must work very hard to accomplish this dream.

Refer to page 236 for one possible revision.

Practice makes permanent

Using commas to make your writing flow will dramatically improve your writing style. As with all the other Painless Techniques, honing your new skill and making it a permanent part of your style should be your ultimate goal. Try the following, on a regular basis, to keep your technique sharp and part of your permanent writing style.

1. Using a previous writing assignment, examine it for comma misuse. Also, examine whether there are short, choppy

sentences that could be combined into a longer, flowing sentence by using the methods of this chapter's Painless Technique.

2. Select a passage from an exciting book that you have read. Notice how the author used commas to create flowing sentences.

Creating readable rhythm

The techniques you mastered will add both power and grace to your writing. As such, you should feel comfortable writing long, flowing sentences. The next chapter will further improve your writing by mixing these flowing sentences into a readable rhythm.

CHAPTER SEVEN

Add Rhythm to Your Writing

CHANGE YOUR PACE
TO KEEP THEM READING

A writing style characterized by sameness in sentence length, type, and structure produces a monotonous essay guaranteed to bore even the most receptive reader. Whenever you write with same-length sentences, particularly sentences that are all very long or very short, your reader loses interest. Long sentences drone on and cause readers to forget the first part of the sentence by the time they reach the sentence's end. Conversely, as we noted in the previous chapter, a composition riddled with short sentences reads like a grade school primer. To avoid this unhappy result, keep your writing interesting; one key to interesting writing is changing your pace throughout the composition by varying the length, type, and structure of your sentences.

Painless Technique

PAINLESS TECHNIQUE NO. 7: VARY THE TYPE, LENGTH, AND STRUCTURE OF YOUR SENTENCES TO ADD RHYTHM TO YOUR WRITING.

If you change your writing's pace, you will give it the necessary rhythm to keep your readers interested. The way to create this rhythm is by blending sentences. Before we see how to blend varying length sentences to make our writing interesting, let us review simple, compound, complex, and compound-complex sentences so that we can see where we are going.

VARY SENTENCE LENGTH

If you calculated the average sentence length of a well-written essay, it would total between 12 and 15 words. You would also notice that the writer included some sentences that were much longer, and some sentences that were much shorter. By using sentences of varying lengths, you will weave simple, compound, complex, and compound-complex sentences together to tell the story.

Let us examine two simple methods for varying sentence length. The first method entails following a long compound or complex sentence with a punchy, short sentence. The example below demonstrates how varying the sentence length adds a rhythm to the writing that keeps it interesting.

POOR

College Bound

John's older brother planned for his college education like a general plans a beach assault. He left nothing to chance and tried thinking of every possible resource. He wanted to assure himself admission into the hallowed halls of Princeton. Sometimes, he thought he should join the army rather than enroll at that center of learning.

Notice that all of the sentences in this passage are nearly the same length. Consequently, the passage provides information, but not in a very interesting fashion. Let's see how we can improve *College Bound*.

BETTER

College Bound

John's older brother planned for his college education like a general plans a beach assault, leaving nothing to chance and thinking of every possible resource to assure himself admission into the hallowed halls of an Ivy League center of learning. On the other hand, he could join the army!

Strive for an average sentence length of 12 to 15 words for your entire essay, and create rhythm by mixing longer and shorter sentences.

Notice that the first sentence is 40 words long, whereas the second sentence is only 9 words long. The abrupt ending emphasizes the alternative career choice, and creates an element of surprise. This method of interspersing a short sentence among long sentences is an easy way to add rhythm to your writing.

Surf's up...

For more information on varying the length of the sentences to improve your writing submissions:

ccc.commnet.edu/grammar/sentences.htm

BRAIN TICKLERS
Set # 37

Write a four-sentence paragraph on any subject by using three long sentences and one short sentence to establish rhythm in the paragraph.

Refer to page 236 for an example.

Let's look at another way to vary the sentence length throughout your writing. The next example illustrates three short sentences counterbalancing a long opening sentence.

POOR

The Athlete

Twenty years later, John took stock of his once sleek, muscled body. It was a body that had flowed so effortlessly up and down the basketball court. He had played basketball for four glorious years. His stomach now looked like he had swallowed a basketball. His hands ached with arthritis. He was winded after walking up a flight of steps.

Again, this passage states information much as an encyclopedia does; however, we want to do more than just present information. We want to involve the reader, and to do that we must keep the reader interested. Let's see how we can add a little rhythm to *The Athlete*.

BETTER

The Athlete

Twenty years later, John took stock of the once sleek, muscled body that had flowed so effortlessly up and down the basketball

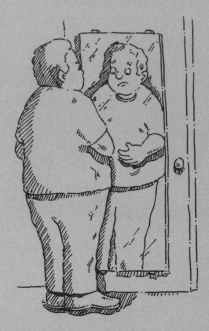

court for four glorious years. His stomach looked like he had swallowed a basketball. His hands ached with arthritis. Walking up a flight of steps winded him.

The opening sentence contains twenty-seven words, whereas the last three sentences each contain nine words or fewer. Notice how effectively the short sentences contrast the opening sentence. Work through the following exercise to practice this sentence length varying technique.

FRAGMENTS CAN CREATE RHYTHM

Using non-sentences or sentence fragments is another effective rhythm-generating technique. Inserting a sentence fragment provides an excellent way to make a point, especially whenever the fragment follows a long, complex sentence. Nevertheless, restrict your use of fragments to your creative writing pieces because they are out of place in a scientific paper.

> **Avoid using sentence fragments to help create rhythm in your writing if you suspect that your reader wants you to write with only complete sentences, even in creative pieces.**

The following example demonstrates how using sentence fragments can add life to a passage. First, read the passage written with sentences of nearly equal length.

POOR

The Room

Mary slowly opened the door into the dark room. Fear was numbing her body and making it hard for her to concentrate. She wanted to run away from the dark room, but she could not make herself move. Taking a deep breath, she felt for the light switch next to the doorframe and flicked it. The light filled the once dark room and Mary looked everywhere, but she did not see anything.

The passage probably does not create the suspense the author desires. However, we can create suspense by writing with long, complex sentences and then slipping in a fragment at just the right moment.

BETTER

The Room

Mary slowly opened the door into the dark room. Fear was numbing her body and making it hard for her to concentrate. She

wanted to run away from the dark room, but she couldn't. Taking a deep breath, she felt for the light switch next to the doorframe and flicked it. Nothing.

Try the following exercise that will help you use fragments to add rhythm to your writing.

BRAIN TICKLERS
Set # 39

Write a five-sentence paragraph on any subject using four long sentences and one sentence fragment to establish rhythm in the paragraph.

Refer to page 237 for an example paragraph.

AVOID SENTENCES WRITTEN IN THE SAME FORM

Sameness with respect to sentence length and paragraph length is not the only villain responsible for monotonous writing. Sentences all written in the same form also create a monotonous passage. For instance, writing with only declarative sentences, especially short declarative sentences in the typical subject-verb-object form, will also cause a reader's eyes to glaze over. Let us examine how we can address this common writing fault.

Vary your sentence openings

The struggling writer rarely deviates from the standard subject-verb-object sentence form. Arguably, the majority of your sentences should be in this form because this style creates a logical flow of events. However, it is the occasional nonstandard sentence or two that sets up a potent left-to-right sentence. As with sentence length, too many sentences written in the same form can lead to monotonous reading, but thankfully, this is an easy fault to correct.

Since the beginning often determines the sentence's form, become aware of the different ways to open sentences. Instead of starting every sentence with a noun used as a subject and then following it with a verb and object, delay introducing the subject by opening your sentence with something other than the subject. The following examples illustrate alternate forms of sentences available to combat the monotony created by endless left-to-right sentences.

Verb before the subject

Instead of writing the following conventionally structured sentences:

> Many students are in Ms. Webster's class.
> The semester is over today.

Begin the sentences with a *verb*, so they now read:

> There *are* many students in Ms. Webster's class.
> Today *is* the end of the semester.

Open with an adverb

Instead of writing the following sentences in the typical subject-verb-object form:

> They sat silently as their writing teacher read their essays.
> The sun set quickly in the western sky.

begin the sentence with an adverb:

> *Silently*, they sat as their writing teacher read their essays.
> *Quickly*, the sun set in the western sky.

Switch the noun and the direct object

Rather than composing sentences that lead off with the subject:

> Mary had seen the writing teacher this morning.
> The students placed their exams on the teacher's desk.

start the sentence with a *direct object*:

> *The writing teacher* was seen by Mary this morning.
> *The exams* were placed on the teacher's desk.

Remind yourself to use this method sparingly because this will create a sentence in the passive. Although passive voice sentences are fine, they take the action away from the subject, so use them only on occasion. If you need to review the passive voice, refer to Chapter Three.

Open with an adjective

Rather than writing the standard subject-verb-object sentence:

> She was angry and frustrated as she stared at the grade on her term paper.
> Maria felt overwhelmed as she continued working on her term paper.

begin the sentence with the *subject's modifying words*:

> *Angry* and *frustrated,* she stared at the grade on her term paper.

> *Overwhelmed,* Maria continued working on her term paper.

Lead with a prepositional phrase

Instead of introducing the sentence with the subject, *she*:

> She hoped the solution to her problem was in this classroom.

begin the sentence with a *prepositional phrase*:

> *In this classroom*, she hoped was the solution to her problem.

Go with a gerund

Rather than writing the standard left-to-right sentence:

> Mary has a goal of writing well.

begin the sentence with a *gerund*:

> *Writing* well is Mary's goal.

The preceding examples should provide you with some ideas for varying your sentence forms. Every so often, give standard left-to-right sentences a rest by substituting one of the above forms in your writing. The following exercise provides an opportunity for you to practice this technique.

BRAIN TICKLERS
Set # 40

Alter the beginning of each sentence so that the sentence is no longer in the subject-verb-object form.

1. The students argued the entire day about where to go on their class trip.

2. The coach was surprised that his team won its last five games.

3. The students learned many of life's lessons in Mr. Greene's classroom.

4. The mother lovingly picked up her new-born baby.

5. The problem can be solved in a number of ways.

6. John lives to climb mountains and back-pack.

7. He was upset that his story was not pub-lished, and so he quit writing.

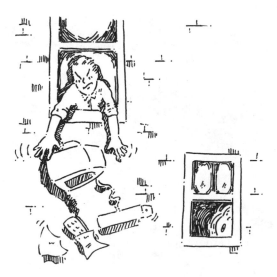

8. Martha is the best writer in the class.

9. The students enjoyed the guest speaker's stories about his travels abroad.

10. John had written the paper that earned him an A in less than 20 minutes.

Refer to pages 237–238 for some possible revisions of these sentences.

Vary the kinds of sentences

The final way to add rhythm to your writing is to vary the types of sentences. Monotony may set in whenever you write sentence after sentence in the declarative. We have seen before that a monotonous passage is a good way to start your reader skimming. While most of your sentences should be declarative, you should occasionally use other types of sentences; an occasional question, exclamation, or command will relieve the declarative monotony. To understand what we are talking about, first read the following paragraph written in the declarative.

POOR

Our class apprehensively waited for Ms. Martin to return our essays. She asked us to raise our hands if we thought we had done a good job writing our essay. She appeared surprised that no one raised his or her hand. She passed the papers back, and when she was finished, she raised her hand. She shouted that everyone had done a terrific job!

Next, read a paragraph that breaks the above paragraph out of the purely declarative mode. Notice that by breaking out of the declarative-only mode, the writer was able to make use of a dialogue.

BETTER

> Our class apprehensively waited for Ms. Martin to return our essays.
>
> "Raise your hand if you thought you did a good job on your essay," she commanded. "No one thinks he or she did a good job?"
>
> She passed the papers back, and when she was finished, she raised her hand and shouted, "I think everyone did a terrific job!"

Did you notice how the interrogative and the exclamation style sentences deliver more snap to the paragraph and bring the reader closer to the story's action and the characters' feelings? However, be wary:

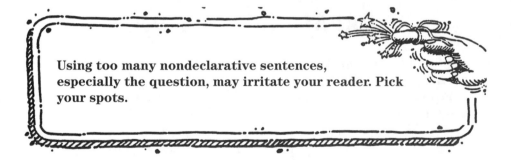

Using too many nondeclarative sentences, especially the question, may irritate your reader. Pick your spots.

The following exercise provides you with an opportunity to write a short passage using the above method.

BRAIN TICKLERS
Set # 41

Compose a multiple paragraph passage where some of the sentences are not written in the declarative.

Refer to page 238 for a sample passage.

PARAGRAPHS CREATE RHYTHM TOO

Differing paragraph length also generates rhythm within your writing submission. For instance, a one-sentence paragraph like the one in the following excerpt is a great way to make your point.

Forget Something?

College life was everything Mary had expected it to be: the mind-challenging courses, new friends, and of course, the odd professor or two, the oddest of whom was Dr. Freeman, her instructor for physics. By all accounts, he was a brilliant professor, but quite absent-minded. Last Tuesday, he was a few minutes into his lecture on angular momentum, when suddenly, his wife burst into the auditorium and interrupted him mid-sentence.

"You forgot your pants!"

The following exercise provides an opportunity to create a rhythm with your paragraphs.

BRAIN TICKLERS
Set # 42

Write two or more paragraphs on any subject. Contrast the length of one of the paragraphs to provide emphasis to your writing.

Refer to page 238 for a sample passage.

Talk to yourself

Look for ways to add rhythm to your writing by varying the length of your sentences and paragraphs, by varying the openings of your sentences, and finally, by varying the types of sentences in your writing submission. Your reader will appreciate the change of pace.

An excellent way to determine whether there is a rhythm to your writing submission is to read it aloud. If you are droning along as you read, use the technique of this chapter to give it some snap. Conversely, if it sounds great as you read aloud, you have done well. Try using this chapter's Painless Technique to add some rhythm to the bland paragraph on page 171. Remember to vary the length, openings, and type of the sentences.

BRAIN TICKLERS
Set # 43

Use the methods of this chapter's Painless Technique to provide some rhythm to the paragraph entitled *Stranded* below.

Stranded

This week of school was finally over. I was glad of that. I was now planning my well-deserved weekend. My best friend, Frank, wanted me to go with him to the beach. He said his brother would drive us to the beach in his 1989 Toyota. I had asked him if he was sure his car could even make it all the way across town. He said that he was sure it could make it to the beach, but he was not as confident that it would bring us home. I suppose there are worse places to be stranded than on the white beaches of Florida.

Refer to page 239 for a suggested paragraph.

Surf's up...

Surf into this site for more information on writing with rhythm:

www.galactic-guide.com/articles/6R62.html

Practice makes permanent

This chapter's Painless Technique is a simple but powerful one. Sentence after sentence and paragraph after paragraph of the same length and type will detract from your hard work. By learning this chapter's Painless Technique for adding rhythm to your writing, you will dramatically improve your submissions. As always, honing your new skill and making it a permanent part of your style should be your ultimate goal. Try the following, perhaps once a day, to keep this technique sharp.

1. Using a previous writing assignment, examine it for sentence sameness. Pull out a paragraph or two, and use your newly learned technique to make the excerpt flow better.

2. Select three or four nonconsecutive paragraphs from a magazine article. Use the methods described in this chapter and give the paragraphs more rhythm.

3. Pull a sample of your most recent writing. Calculate the average sentence length for a few paragraphs. Now, select an excerpt of what you feel is good writing. Calculate the excerpt's average sentence length. Any difference?

Adding some polish

The Painless Techniques that you have learned thus far will improve your writing, and you should notice this improvement over a short period of time. This next Painless Technique will polish your now strong writing by making you aware of some commonly misused words that detract from your work.

CHAPTER EIGHT

Gremlins in Your Writing

REPEAT OFFENDERS

Some writers consistently misuse certain words. Unfortunately, misusing words detracts from the authority and hard work of the author because the reader focuses on the writing mistake and ignores the writer's message. It's not fair, but that is the way it happens all too often. You can prevent this from occurring by using these commonly misused words properly.

Painless Technique

PAINLESS TECHNIQUE NO. 8: LEARN THE PROPER USAGE OF COMMONLY MISUSED WORDS.

THE TOP TEN GREMLINS

Below are the top ten gremlins, that is, the ten most commonly misused sets of words. To avoid bringing negative attention to your writing, make sure that you understand when to use them.

> affect/effect
> altogether/all together
> infer/imply
> lay/lie
> disinterested/uninterested
> sit/set
> who/which/that
> fewer/less
> principal/principle
> who/whom

Let's take a look at these potential grade destroyers.

Gremlin set no. 1: affect/effect

This first set of gremlins causes even the most careful writers to slip up once in a while. The verb *affect* means "to make an impression on, to influence." By contrast, the word *effect* can act as a noun or a verb. When acting as a noun, *effect* means "the result produced by a cause." When the word acts as a verb, it means, "to cause or to bring about." Notice their use in the example below.

WRONG

Poor writing will *effect* your grade.

The coach slammed his hand of the table for *affect*.

The rainstorm *affected* a delay in our arrival.

Notice that in the first sentence the author is telling us that poor writing will have a negative influence on your grade; therefore, we need to use *affect*, rather than *effect*. Similarly, in the second sentence, the coach is slamming his hand to impress something upon the players; thus, *effect* is the proper word in this instance. Finally, in our last sentence, the consequence of the rainstorm is a late arrival. This means that we use *effected*, rather than *affected*.

RIGHT

Poor writing will adversely *affect* your grade.

The coach slammed his hand on the table for *effect*.

The rainstorm *effected* a delay in our arrival.

Gremlin set no. 2: altogether/all together

This is another gremlin couple that brings out the teacher's red correction pen, but once we understand their definitions, these words should not give any trouble. *Altogether* means "completely, thoroughly." *All together* means "as a group." Let's see how they apply in the following sentences.

WRONG

Your answer in class was *all together* wrong.

Altogether, the class answered the question incorrectly.

The first sentence is informing us that the answer was completely wrong; therefore, we need to use *altogether*. In writing the second sentence, the author is informing us that, as a group, the class answered incorrectly. To write the sentence correctly, we must use *all together*.

RIGHT

Your answer in class was *altogether* wrong.

All together, the class answered the question incorrectly.

Another set of gremlins bites the dust! Pretty easy so far, right? But don't become overconfident—the next set can be tricky.

Gremlin set no. 3: infer/imply

The word *infer* means "to arrive at by reasoning" or "to deduce." Contrast this usage to the word *imply*, which means "to suggest or hint."

WRONG

I *implied* that I would have trouble passing the class when the teacher returned my exam with a red F on it.

I had *inferred* that I liked Mary Ellen, but I was too shy to do anything about it.

The first sentence is telling us that the student has deduced that he will have trouble passing the class because he earned an F on the midterm; therefore, we must use the word *infer* to get this point across. In the second sentence, the author is hinting that he liked Mary Ellen but was too shy to do anything about it; therefore, this sentence requires that we use *implied*.

RIGHT

I *inferred* that I would have trouble passing the class when the teacher returned my exam with a red F on it.

I had *implied* that I liked Mary Ellen, but I was too shy to do anything about it.

These sets of gremlins should not give you any trouble and now you will be able to use them with confidence in your writing. To make sure this is the case, the following exercise provides an opportunity to apply what you have learned.

BRAIN TICKLERS
Set # 44

Select the proper word for each of the following sentences.

1. We left (altogether, all together).

2. From his tone of voice, I (inferred, implied) that he was upset and angry.

3. How do the clouds (affect, effect) the temperature?

4. I felt (altogether, all together) out of place at the party on Saturday night.

5. The (inference, implication) taken from the fact that there are no school buses in front of school is that we will not be going on the class trip.

6. The Boy Scouts were not (affected, effected) by rain as they hiked through the hills of central Texas.

7. I am not (all together, altogether) sure why we are here.

8. Are you (inferring, implying) that I write poorly?

9. Such a statement could have a serious, long-term (affect, effect) on me.

(Answers are on page 239.)

You should feel pretty confident that you could keep these three sets of gremlins under control in your writing. Now let's move on to the fourth gremlin set.

Gremlin set no. 4: lay/lie

When to use *lay* or *lie* is relatively easy once you are aware of the definition of each word. To *lay* means "to put or place in a more or less horizontal position." Conversely, the phrase *to lie* means "to recline."

Most students know this, but they confuse themselves when they move away from the present tense. Listed below are the principal parts of these troublesome words:

Present	lay	lie
Past	laid	lay
Present Participle	laying	lying
Past Participle	laid	lain

Remember that *lay* requires a direct object; you always lay something. However, you never lie anything; you just *lie* down.

WRONG

Matt *lied* the blanket over the sleeping children.

Katie was *laying* on the new sofa.

In the first sentence, the subject, *Matt*, is placing the blanket in a horizontal position over the direct object, *the sleeping children*. Consequently, to write the sentence properly, we need to use the verb, *laid*. In the next sentence, the subject, *Katie*, is reclining on the new sofa, which means that we must write the sentence with the verb, *lying*.

RIGHT

Matt *laid* the blanket over the sleeping children.

Katie was *lying* on the new sofa.

The next words are a particularly tricky set for some writers. Take your time, and make sure you understand when to use each word. Remember, these examples are always here for your review. However, it is really not that difficult to tell these gremlins apart. Let's take a look at them.

Gremlin set no. 5: disinterested/uninterested

The distinction between these two words eludes many writers. The word *disinterested* means "unbiased" or "neutral." By contrast, *uninterested* means "not interested" or "bored."

WRONG

Ms. Smith was appointed as a judge for the trial because she was an *uninterested* party.

The football team was so far behind that it was *disinterested* in the halftime speech of its coach.

The writer means that Ms. Smith was appointed as a judge because she was unbiased, not because she did not care; therefore, we should describe Ms. Smith as a *disinterested* party. By contrast, the football team is not unbiased; it is aloof toward its coach. To properly describe the team's spirit, it is necessary to use *uninterested*.

RIGHT

He was appointed as a judge for the trial because he was a *disinterested* party.

The football team was so far behind that it was *uninterested* in the halftime speech of its coach.

We have almost finished. Now let's move on, and tackle those pesky sit/set gremlins.

Surf's up...

Check out this site to help you keep an annoying gremlin from ruining your writing:

members.home.net/englishzone/verbs/lie-lay.html

Gremlin set no. 6: sit/set

This is another word set that confuses students when they move from the present tense; therefore, we will examine the other tenses so that we are no longer confused. The principal parts of these two verbs are:

Present	sit	set
Past	sat	set
Past Participle	sat	set
Present Participle	sitting	setting

People *sit*, whereas you *set* something—with the following exceptions: the sun sets, concrete sets.

WRONG

Clara *set* at her usual place at dinner.

My brother *sat* the table for dinner.

Since Clara is a person, she *sits* at the table. In the first sentence, therefore, we must use *sat* rather than *set* to write the sentence properly. By contrast, the second sentence tries to describe the brother's action of preparing the table, and to do that he must place silverware and plates on the table. The verb that describes this action is *set*.

RIGHT

Clara *sat* at her usual place at dinner.

My brother *sets* the table for dinner.

Surf's up...

There is help in cyberspace if you need it to keep the gremlins at bay:

www.romance-central.com/workshops/gram.htm

Before we move on, work through the following exercise to make sure that you can use these word sets.

BRAIN TICKLERS
Set # 45

Select the proper word for each sentence.

1. The competition became so boring that the (disinterested, uninterested) judge also soon became (disinterested, uninterested).

2. The dog (set, sat) on the car to keep warm.

3. I will just (lie, lay) the blanket down over here.

4. (Lie, lay) down on the bed in my room.

5. The Spirit Club arrived early to (set, sit) up the refreshments for the pep rally.

6. John was (lying, laying) asleep across the lab table.

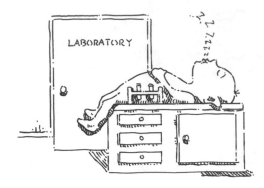

7. (Sit, Set) down!

8. My brother is always (lying, laying) on the sofa.

9. The nurse had (lain, laid) a blanket over the shivering patient.

10. John was so (disinterested, uninterested) in the class that he fell asleep.

(Answers are on page 240.)

Now we are ready to tackle some triplet gremlins. These confuse many writers, but by the time we have finished, you will never have a problem.

Gremlin set no. 7: who/which/that

Use the word *who* when you want to refer to people or to animals (that you want to personify). By contrast, use *which* to refer to animals or inanimate objects. Finally, you can use *that* to refer to either people or things.

WRONG

I am the student *which* signed up for the swimming lesson.

The food *who* is sitting on the table is rotten.

The writer *which* signed up for the class is Jim.

Since *the student* obviously refers to a person, in the first sentence we must use the word *who* to refer to the student. In the following sentence, *the rotten pieces of food* are inanimate objects; therefore, we need to use the word *which* or *that* to refer to them. Finally, the subject, *writer*, in the third sentence is a person. This means that we need to use either *who* or *that* to refer to that person.

RIGHT

I am the student *who* signed up for the swimming lesson.

The food, *which* is sitting on the table, is rotten.

or

The food *that* is sitting on the table is rotten.

The writer *who* signed up for the class is Jim.

or

The writer *that* signed up for the class is Jim.

That was a rather difficult set, but this next set of gremlins should give you less problems—or is it fewer problems?

Gremlin set no. 8: fewer/less

Writers frequently misuse *fewer* and *less*. Let's examine these words and see when to use them. To begin, you should use *fewer* to refer to objects that can be counted, whereas *less* should be used to refer to qualities or concepts that cannot be counted.

WRONG

Mary received *less* A's on her semester report card than you.

I suppose that is because I have *fewer* determination.

Since Mary is able to count the number of A's on her semester report card, the writer should use *fewer* to describe the situation, rather than *less*, whereas in the second sentence, determination cannot be counted; therefore, the writer should not use *fewer* to describe the level of determination. Instead, *less* should be used to describe the amount of determination.

RIGHT

I received *fewer* A's on my semester report card than you.

I suppose that is because I have *less* determination.

The next set of gremlins confuses many writers, but it is very easy to choose correctly. Let's see how.

Gremlin set no. 9: principal/principle

The concept is a straightforward one. Use the word *principal* when referring to the principal of a school, the principal person in a movie, the principal cause, or the principal remaining on a loan. In contrast, the word *principle* means "rule or essential truth." Remember, we should live our lives by *principles*, and be respectful of the *principal* of the school.

WRONG

"Work hard" is my guiding *principal*.

The *principle* told me that I needed to work harder.

In the first sentence, the writer is referring to a standard or a code for conducting her life; therefore, *principle* is the proper word to use in this sentence. In the second sentence, a person is urging the writer to work harder, which means the writer must use *principal* to refer to this person.

RIGHT

"Work hard" is my guiding *principle*.

The *principal* told me that I needed to work harder.

One last set to go! Unfortunately, it is a tough one for a lot of writers.

Gremlin set 10: who/whom

There are two main situations where these words occur. The first is where they begin subordinate clauses, and the other is where they begin questions. Let us first examine the subordinate clause situation.

In subordinate clauses, whether we use *who* or *whom* depends upon what the subordinate clause refers to. Use *who* if you are referring to the subject of the clause. Conversely, use *whom* if you are referring to the object of the clause.

WRONG

The boys *whom* failed the test did not study.

RIGHT

The boys *who* failed the test did not study.

Who begins the subordinate clause "failed the test" and that describes the subject "the boys."

Now look at the next set.

WRONG

Who are you driving to school?

The subject of the sentence is *you*. The person being driven is receiving the action and is, therefore, the object. This being the case, we must use *whom* in the sentence.

RIGHT

Whom are you driving to school?

The rule regarding these words in questions is rather simple: If the question refers to the subject of the sentence, then choose *who*. If the question refers to the object of the sentence, then choose *whom*. The following examples illustrate this rule.

Who wrote this essay?

Notice that *who* refers to the subject of the sentence.

Whom does the article refer to?

Whom receives the referring; the article does the referring. Therefore, whom is correctly used here because it refers to the direct object.

Surf's up...

Here are a couple of sites that you can refer to so that your writing is gremlin-free:

ccc.commnet.edu/grammar/notorious/that.htm
www.protrainco.com/info/essays/pronouns.htm

Those gremlins should give you no problems now; however, just to make sure they will not, try the exercises below.

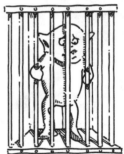

BRAIN TICKLERS
Set # 46

Choose the correct word in each of the following sentences.

1. The (principal, principle) reason we lost the game was my fumble at the one-yard line.

2. He had (fewer, less) bruises on his body than I did.

3. The author (which, who, that) wrote this book is very talented.

4. (Who/Whom) is your favorite author?

5. John, to (who/whom) I am related, is attending the class.

6. The (principal, principle) always attended every football game.

7. The (least, fewest) amount of time will be wasted if we walk rather than wait for the bus.

(Answers are on page 240.)

Practice makes permanent

Properly using these ten sets of word gremlins will keep your reader focused on the content of your writing. As with all the other Painless Techniques, honing your new skill and making it a permanent part of your style should be your ultimate goal. Try the following, on a regular basis, to keep your technique sharp and part of your permanent writing style.

1. Using a previous writing assignment, examine it for misuse of the ten problem sets of words.

2. Once a day, select a problem set and write a sentence or two using the words. Work your way through all ten sets, and then start over.

YOU HAVE STYLE, SUBSTANCE, AND GRACE

When properly employed, the eight techniques presented in this book will dramatically improve your writing by imparting a sense of style and grace to your writing, as well as making it more interesting and substantive for your reader. The last technique is a targeted technique. Its target is the dreaded term paper.

CHAPTER NINE

Create a Template
for Your Term Paper

THE FRAMEWORK FOR SUCCESS

This year may be the first time that you are asked to write a term paper; therefore, it is important for you to understand how to confront this task and subsequently produce a quality paper. However, let's first look at the process from the teacher's point of view.

A teacher will assign a term paper, usually five to ten double-spaced pages in length, to encourage you to learn more about a particular topic covered by the course and to think more critically about that topic within the subject matter of the course. A good term paper from a teacher's point of view, therefore, is more than just transferring facts from various sources to your paper. Rather, it is your well thought-out analysis of certain key issues related to the topic. Before we see how this chapter's Painless Technique will help you to write a paper that meets this criterion, let's look at the very important first step that is often not considered enough by writers.

First things, first—selecting a topic

Your teacher may assign your term paper topic; however, if he or she lets you choose your own topic, there are a few things that you should consider. These are listed below in order of importance.

1. Availability of materials.

Make sure the topic that you are considering has an adequate amount of reference material readily available. This reference material should include sources from recently published books, recent articles from scholarly magazines, and information from currently updated web sites hosted by universities or similar scholarly organizations.

Note: Keep a good record of the materials that you use or plan to use so that you will be able to compile a bibliography.

2. Level of complexity of the topic.

Your topic should challenge you, rather than overwhelm or confuse you. As you are researching various topics, eliminate the ones that are just too complex for you. You won't impress your teacher by turning in page after page of information that

he or she knows you do not understand. Remember that you must not only provide facts about your topic, but you must analyze important issues attributable to that topic as well. Consequently, an overly difficult topic will not allow you to fulfill both of these requirements. Similarly, do not choose a topic that is below your understanding level because the object of the term paper is to provide you with an opportunity to learn more about a topic that interests you.

3. What is the rest of the class doing?

    Take note of what your classmates are considering for their topics. Be different. Your teacher will appreciate the variety, and that you are the one providing it. Of course, remember to stay within the topic limits that your teacher had provided. Discuss the topic with your parents or other adults who will give you an honest opinion, and whose tastes may be fairly close to those of your teacher.

    Whether the teacher assigns the topic or grants you the freedom to select a topic within the range of the course material, what will distinguish your paper will be how coherently you discuss the topic and how well your research supports your assertions of fact and opinion. With this in mind, the term paper or research paper need not be an overwhelming task; your teacher means for it to be challenging, but not overwhelming.

Surf's up...

The following site discusses
how to pick a term paper topic:

www.aci-plus.com/tips/tips4.htm

THE *POWER* TEMPLATE

To keep from becoming immediately overwhelmed by this challenging task, you need to, as quickly as possible, fit the paper's topic into a research paper template. This chapter's Painless Technique addresses how you can successfully use this template to create a quality term paper without wasting a lot of time and effort. Be aware, however, that creating a quality term paper takes time and effort; this technique will help you to be efficient with both.

We are now ready to use the *POWER* template. Once you have narrowed your initial research down to choose a topic (or it has been chosen for you), now it is time to fit your topic into the *POWER* template.

Painless Technique

PAINLESS TECHNIQUE NO. 9: USE A *POWER* TEMPLATE TO CREATE A QUALITY RESEARCH PAPER.

The proposition statement

We begin this template process with the letter "P," the first letter in the *POWER* template. Once you have selected a topic, write a one-sentence statement about it. This Painless Technique refers to the one-sentence exposition that concisely summarizes the entire paper as a *proposition statement.* The proposition, or *thesis statement* as it is also known, should focus your research and provide direction for your paper. It should set out what you propose to write about. Moreover, it is important to design a proposition statement to narrow the focus of your paper; if you cannot explain your proposed paper topic in one sentence, you probably do not have a clear idea of what you want to write about.

As you embark on your preliminary research, you may find that you need to revise your proposition statement to support your research. This process of researching and revising is a necessary process for establishing the framework within which to write your paper. However, a note of caution:

> The proposition statement is a vital component of the research paper; do not modify a well-thought-out proposition statement because you have not done sufficient research to support it. Do the research.

Finally, ask yourself whether your proposition statement interests you enough to read further. Obviously, if it doesn't sound very interesting to you, it probably will not be for your teacher either. As a further check, ask your parents or some

other adults; notice how they react to your proposition statement. Now, let's look at how to create a winning proposition statement.

Surf's up...

Refer to these sites if you need more help writing a proposition statement:

www.aci-plus.com/tips/tips5.htm
ccc.commnet.edu/grammar/composition/thesis.htm

The following example sets forth the process for constructing the proposition statement. Remember, however, that it must be succinct enough to fit into a single sentence.

EXAMPLE 1

A student in a history class has decided to write about some facet of the tragedy of the Holocaust. More specifically, she has decided to write about the efforts of German citizens to save the lives of Jews during the reign of Adolf Hitler; a working title for her paper is *Heroes of the Holocaust*. One possible proposition statement for this research paper is:

Proposition Statement for *Heroes of the Holocaust*

> Germans of all backgrounds, occupations, and religions risked their own safety to aid Jews hiding or escaping from the Nazis.

Notice how the proposition statement provides direction to the paper by stating that the paper will dwell on the unlikely hero, rather than the courageous soldier in battle. Moreover, the proposition statement focuses this writer's efforts on discussing those Germans who bravely aided the Jews, as compared to people who risked their lives for other peoples or causes. Do not undervalue this effect of the proposition statement to focus the writer's effort. A serious problem encountered by writers inexperienced at preparing research papers is that they approach the assignment with much too broad a proposition statement. Consequently, it becomes difficult for them to write a paper from which they can analyze and draw conclusions from their research. That is why it is important to get your paper off to a good start with a workable proposition statement. This next example will depict the effect of a proposition statement.

EXAMPLE 2

A student in a Language Arts class decides to write a term paper about Mark Twain. She has completed some preliminary research and has written two proposition statements. Let's look at them.

POOR

Mark Twain was a great writer and led a very interesting life.

Notice that this proposition statement is rather broad, not to mention not very interesting. This proposition statement will make it very difficult for this author to write a paper and keep it within the five- to ten-page limit.

BETTER
Many of Mark Twain's books were banned from libraries.

Notice how this sentence narrows the discussion to one aspect of Mark Twain's life. By narrowing the topic, the writer can focus her research and write a paper that not only informs, but analyzes as well. In addition, this paper sounds like it will be a lot more interesting.

It takes some practicing to become proficient at writing proposition statements; however, once you learn this skill, you will be writing better term papers. The following exercise will provide you with the opportunity to construct your own proposition statements.

BRAIN TICKLERS
Set # 47

Below are some selected term paper topics. Write a proposition statement for each topic so that the statement helps you establish the direction and the tone of the paper.

1. Who Should Take the Lead in Cleaning Up Polluted Air in Our Large Cities?

2. Is the Internet Creating an Economic Divide?

3. Handguns Should Be Banned in the United States

4. Should Schools Be in Session All Year?

5. Have School Subjects Become Outdated?

6. The Role of Sports in the United States

If you would like to see some suggested proposition statements, refer to page 241.

If necessary, modify your proposition statement

From time to time, as your paper develops and you focus your topic, test the proposition statement against what you have written so far. If necessary, modify your proposition statement as your research indicates. Again, be careful not to change your proposition statement to fit your research if you suspect that you really should do more research.

Once you are satisfied with your proposition statement, you are ready to move to the next section of the template.

Creating the outline

The "O" in *POWER* represents "Outline." Once you have constructed the proposition statement, create a preliminary outline containing main points that will support the proposition statement. As you develop this preliminary outline, try to formulate three points to support your proposition statement. We use three points because most people can easily remember and process three concepts. Any fewer, and it appears that your paper does not adequately cover the topic; more points will only overwhelm your readers so that they will ignore or simply forget one or two of them. Assign each point its own section in the outline, keeping in mind that each supporting element must buttress the main idea. Keep the amount you write on each point roughly proportional to the importance of that idea. Do not be too critical as you get the points on paper for the first time.

The outline should help you organize research and writing so that it addresses the proposition or thesis of your paper. Once you have established your three points, you can focus your research a bit more. Obviously, as you continue your research, you may need to adjust one or more of your three main points. Remember, however, that no matter what type of revision, the main points must always support the proposition statement.

Let us return to our Example 1 topic, *Heroes of the Holocaust.* The following is one possibility for a three-point outline supporting the topic's proposition statement. First, the proposition statement:

Proposition Statement:

> Germans of all backgrounds, occupations, and religions risked their own safety to aid Jews hiding or escaping from the Nazis.

Next, we build our outline from the research we have done so far. Notice that the outline sets out the three main points that comprise part of the *POWER* template.

Heroes of the Holocaust

I.   Many German citizens risked their lives to hide and smuggle Jews out of the country.

II. Repulsed by the atrocities of their leaders, many German soldiers aided Jews.

III. For years, Jewish leaders continued to show their appreciation for the Germans who helped their people.

Conclusion

Once you have determined the three sections, you can begin filling in the outline with sub-points as your research indicates. The following outline shows how the writer has added sub-points based upon the accumulated research she has done.

I.   Many German citizens risked their lives to hide and smuggle Jews out of the country.
   A.   Anti-semitism in 1930s Germany
   B.   Selected German resistance to anti-semitism
      1. Hiding Jews in their homes
      2. Providing Jews with money and documents to escape

II. Repulsed by the atrocities of their leaders, many German soldiers aided Jews.
   A.   Soldiers "overlook" homes of famous Jews
   B.   Soldiers carry off "dead Jews"

III. For years, Jewish leaders continued to show their appreciation for the Germans who helped their people.
   A.   Letters of appreciation
   B.   Street names in Israel

Conclusion

Alternatively, you can wait and fill in the outline as you learn more from your research. Just make sure you stay within the template and that your research is adequate.

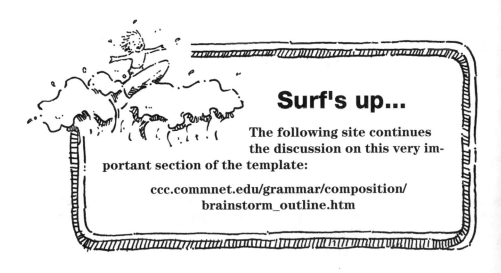

Surf's up...

The following site continues the discussion on this very important section of the template:

**ccc.commnet.edu/grammar/composition/
brainstorm_outline.htm**

Outlining is an important part of the term paper process. It helps reinforce your proposition statement, as well as direct your research. Many students mistakenly believe that they can skip this process to save time. Doing so will cost you more time spent with research in the wrong areas, and it will decrease the quality of your final paper. The following exercise will help you construct the three-point outline, which is a critical piece of your research paper template.

BRAIN TICKLERS
Set # 48

Using the Set # 47 topics set forth below and the proposition statements you wrote, create a three-point outline for the research paper. Assume you have the research information available to support your points.

1. Who Should Take the Lead in Cleaning Up Polluted Air in Our Large Cities?

2. Is the Internet Creating an Economic Divide?

3. Handguns Should Be Banned in the United States

4. Should Schools Be in Session All Year?

5. Have School Subjects Become Outdated?

6. The Role of Sports in the United States

If you would like to see some sample outlines, refer to pages 241–243.

Do not trash your template

This chapter's Painless Technique is a very simple but powerful one; however, it is only powerful if you use it. As you work through the research process, take care to make sure your research is supporting your main points. Don't let inadequate research force you to change your outline. You can avoid this unfortunate situation by starting early on your paper so that you have enough time to research your topic, but do not be afraid to change your outline after doing some research. Your outline before you begin your research is a preliminary one, and your research may direct you to modify or replace some of your points. That is fine, as long as after you have thoroughly researched your topic, you have a  properly constructed outline from which to begin writing your paper. Once your outline is framed up, it is time to move on to the next section of the template.

The rough draft: get those ideas on paper

The "W" in *POWER* stands for "Write." Once you have your proposition statement and detailed outline, it should be an easy task to write a rough draft. Write the first draft with content in mind, rather than concentrating on style. The most important criterion in this part of the template is to get your thoughts down on paper. Remember to always keep checking to see that the draft fits your proposition statement. If you do that, then you can determine whether your research is adequate or if you need to do more in certain areas. Once you have your thoughts down on paper in template form, you are ready for the next step.

A word about plagiarism

Plagiarism is inserting information directly as it is written from a book, magazine article, or web site into your paper without giving credit to its author. When you do this, you give the reader the impression that these are your thoughts rather than those of the author. This is a serious infraction and you must avoid doing this. Many times, teachers will fail the term paper writer for plagiarizing someone's work.

Caution—Major Mistake Territory!

If you wish to take a passage directly from a source, make sure that you attribute that passage to its author in your paper. It is therefore important that you pay close attention to how your teacher wants you to cite or reference your sources. Your teacher should give you some guidelines on how many words the passage must be before it needs to be cited, and how to cite the source.

Rewrite, rewrite, rewrite

The key to a good paper is in the rewriting. As you edit and rewrite your paper, use the techniques presented earlier in this book to create a top-quality research paper. This is where the "E" in *POWER* comes in. It stands for "Enhance." Rewrite not only to improve the writing quality of your paper, but more important, to check your logic and arguments well. This is time well spent, as your teacher will certainly notice the difference between your paper and one that is thrown together at a single writing. Moreover, you

should notice a big difference between your rough draft and your final product.

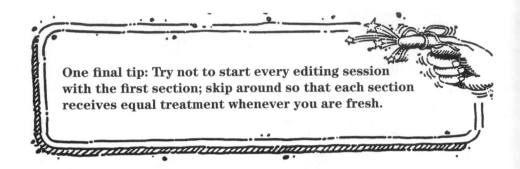

One final tip: Try not to start every editing session with the first section; skip around so that each section receives equal treatment whenever you are fresh.

When you feel you nearly have a final version, let someone else read it. Another pair of eyes and a different point of view will catch many mistakes and help with the logic of the paper. When you are satisfied, and your reader(s) are satisfied, you are finished, almost.

I say almost finished because you have one more section to complete the template. You must construct your bibliography or table of references.

References and citations

Every term paper needs to have a bibliography of sources at the end of it. The final piece of the template is references (the "R" in *POWER*). Teachers look for strong references and a variety of references, especially recent books, in your bibliography. I would like to tell you that there is one correct way to cite references, but the fact is that every teacher thinks that he or she knows the proper form for citing references. Unfortunately, the correct form varies, depending upon the teacher; therefore, pay close attention if your teacher provides you with the format he or she wants for the references. If your teacher has not provided you with a format, below is the standard format for citing books, articles from magazines, and information from web pages. **Note**: If your entry runs more than one line, indent the second and third lines.

- *Citing a book*
  Smith, Lamar. *Term Paper Writing Made Easy*. New York: Writers Press 1998.
- *Citing a magazine article*
  Jones, Margaret, and Sandra Reynolds. "Writing That Term Paper." *Contemporary Writer* 15 April 2000;18–25.
- *Citing an Internet source*
  Jones, Casey. Contemporary American Authors. University of Chicago. 12 December 2000: Available: http://www.uchi/resources/writers.html [12/15/2000]
- *Citing an encyclopedia topic*
  World Book Encyclopedia, 4th ed., s.v. "American Writers."
- *Citing an interview*
  Hemingway, Ernest. Interview by author. Oak Park, Ill., 16 Sept. 1910.

Citing references can be time consuming until you become familiar with the process. The following exercise will help you get acquainted with setting up a bibliography.

BRAIN TICKLERS
Set # 49

The following references were used to write a term paper. Prepare a bibliography for the paper.

1. A book entitled *The Life and Times of an English Teacher*. Pamela Smith authored the book; Random House in New York published it in 1998.

2. An article entitled "Teaching Is My Life." The article is from the June 18, 1999 issue of American Teacher Magazine, pages 45–49. John Saunders wrote the article.

3. A personal interview with Ms. Nancy Ramsey, an English teacher at George Washington Middle School in Dover, Maryland. The interview took place on December 1, 2000.

4. An article entitled "How to Teach English Literature" found on the National Middle School Teachers of America web site. The article was authored by Jayne Freeman on November 30, 1999.

(Answers are on pages 243–244.)

Surf's up...

This site offers some more insight into creating a bibliography:

www.gened.arizona.edu/gonzalez/writing.htm

Practice makes permanent

This chapter's Painless Technique is a simple, but powerful one to improve the quality of your term papers. Obviously, you do not write term papers on a daily basis—although it sometimes may seem like it! This makes it hard to sharpen this chapter's Painless Technique so that you have it at your disposal whenever you need it. Therefore, we must look for opportunities to practice this very important technique. Try the following, perhaps weekly, to keep this technique sharp.

1. Using a previous term paper, develop a proposition statement and three-point outline for the topic. Do you feel that if you were to write this paper now, it would be better?

2. Select an article that is similar to a term paper from a top rated magazine. Develop a proposition statement and three-point outline for the article.

IT'S UP TO YOU!

Make these Painless Techniques an integral part of your writing. Practice them every time you write a term paper, composition, or note on the refrigerator. Within a short time, they will be second nature and you can confidently write any assignment.

Keep this book at your desk or carry it with you so that if you ever need to review one of the techniques, it will be handy. Good luck and good writing!

APPENDIX—FURTHER READING

Aitchison, James. *The Cassell Guide to Written English*. New York: Sterling Publishing, 1999.

Axelrod, Rise, and Charles Cooper. *The St. Martin's Guide to Writing*. Fifth Edition. New York: St. Martin's Press, 1997.

Fulwiler, Toby, and Alan Hayakawa. *The Blair Handbook*. Second Edition. Upper Saddle River: Blair Press, 1997.

Greenbaum, Sidney. *A College Grammar of English*. New York: Longman, Inc., 1989.

Hairston, Maxine, and John Ruskiewicz. *The Scott, Foresman Handbook for Writers*. Second Edition. New York: HarperCollins Publishers, 1991.

Kemper, Dave. *Writers Express*. Burlington: Write Source Educational Publishing House, 1995.

Stevens, Mark, and Jocelyn White Franklin. *Meriam-Webster's Concise Handbook*. Second Edition. Springfield: Meriam Webster, Inc., 1998.

Williams, Joseph. *Style: Toward Clarity and Grace*. Chicago: The University of Chicago Press, 1990.

BRAIN TICKLERS—THE ANSWERS

Chapter One

Set # 1, page 8

Exploring Mars

At this point in time, Mars is the target of the modern astronaut. By reason of its relative closeness to Earth, Mars is being studied by scientists for the purposes of a future mission. In a manner similar to the earlier study of the Moon by scientists, a probe is planned to be sent by NASA to within the immediate vicinity of the planet with a view toward collecting data with respect to the atmosphere of the planet. NASA plans to send in excess of one dozen of these probes during the course of the next five years.

From the point of view of a nonscientist, this proposed expenditure of billions of dollars for the purpose of studying an inhospitable planet appears to be a waste of money and human effort. At this point in time, our own planet and its inhabitants are in need of attention, particularly with regard to the environment. However, on the basis of what I have seen thus far, this concern will not be addressed at this point in time or at a point later into the future.

We must not succumb to this attack of viciousness on our common sense. Of course, I am writing in reference to the concerted effort of the community of scientists, the politicians, and the groups with special interests. We must persevere in our quest to bring this question of social importance to the attention of the public.

Set # 2, page 14

1. The Smiths live in the immediate vicinity of our school. (10)
   The Smiths live *near* our school. (6)

2. By virtue of winning the most games during the season, our team earned the home court advantage. (17)
   By winning the most games during the season, our team earned the home court advantage. (15)

3. <u>At this point in time</u>, we are not sure where we are going on vacation. (15)
    We are not sure *now* where we are going on vacation. (11)

4. <u>During the course of our conversation</u>, we decided not to spend <u>in excess of</u> ten dollars. (16)
    During our conversation, we decided not to spend more than ten dollars. (12)

5. He called me <u>in reference to the new class</u> that was forming. (12)
    He called me *about* the new class that was forming. (10)

6. He ate <u>in excess of six doughnuts</u>. (7)
    He ate *more* than six doughnuts. (6)

7. She is calling <u>in relation to the swimming lessons</u>. (9)
    She is calling *about* the swimming lessons. (7)

8. I am <u>in favor of</u> taking another class trip. (8)
    I am *for* taking another class trip. (6)

9. Anna journeyed to Phoenix <u>by means of car</u>. (8)
    Anna journeyed to Phoenix *by* car. (6)

10. I am <u>in receipt of your letter</u>. (7)
    I *received* your letter. (4)

11. <u>During the course of the class</u>, I fell asleep. (9)
    During the class, I fell asleep. (6)

12. He won the contest <u>by means of cheating</u>. (8)
    He won the contest *by* cheating. (6)

13. I live <u>in the immediate vicinity of you</u>. (8)
    I live *near* you. (4)

14. I am <u>in receipt of your note</u>. (7)
    I *have* your note. (4) I *received* your note. (4)

15. I have a question <u>in relation to my final history grade</u>. (11)
    I have a question *about* my final history grade. (9)

Set # 3, page 17

1. <u>With regard to my grade</u>, the teacher was against changing it. (11)
   Regarding my grade, the teacher was against changing it. (9)

2. <u>With a sense of doom</u>, he called for help. (9)
   Sensing doom, he called for help. (6)

3. <u>In his desire to do well</u> in school, John quit playing baseball five days a week. (16)
   Desiring to do well in school, John quit playing baseball five days a week. (14)

4. <u>In a race against time</u>, Sally stayed up all night working on her project. (14)
   Racing against time, Sally stayed up all night working on her project. (12)

5. <u>With an eye on the storm clouds,</u> the family unpacked the picnic basket. (13)
   Eyeing the storm clouds, the family unpacked the picnic basket. (10)

6. <u>Without much concern</u>, Sandy walked down the dimly lit street. (10)
   Unconcerned, Sandy walked down the dimly lit street. (8)

7. <u>In need of money</u>, the students called home. (8)
   Needing money, the students called home. (6)

8. <u>In his hurry</u> to paint the birdhouse, John spilled the paint. (11)
   Hurrying to paint the birdhouse, John spilled the paint. (9)

9. <u>With a lack of common sense</u>, the boys raced the train to the crossing. (14)
   Lacking common sense, the boys raced the train to the crossing. (11)

10. <u>With his lack of manners</u>, he embarrassed everyone seated at the dinner table. (13)

Lacking manners, he embarrassed everyone seated at the dinner table. (10)

11. <u>With the hope of landing a movie part</u>, the young actor studied his lines. (14)
    Hoping to land a movie part, the young actor studied his lines. (12)

12. <u>With a taste of victory</u>, the runner bolted across the finish line. (12)
    Tasting victory, the runner bolted across the finish line. (9)

13. The student, <u>with one eye on the clock</u>, hurried through the test. (12)
    The student, *eyeing* the clock, hurried through the test. (9)

Set # 4, page 20

1. His actions were <u>under close control</u>. (6)
   His actions were *closely* controlled. (5)

2. Her books were <u>under strict censure</u>. (6)
   Her books were *strictly* censured. (5)

3. His speech was comprised <u>of many humble statements</u>. (8)
   His speech was *humbly* stated. (5)

4. John was the victim <u>of a brutal attack</u>. (8)
   John was *brutally* attacked. (4)

5. Janet was <u>under the mistaken assumption</u> that she was not liked. (11)
   Janet *mistakenly* assumed that she was not liked. (8)

6. The senator's remarks were <u>under intense scrutiny</u>. (7)
   The senator's remarks were *intensely* scrutinized. (6)

Set # 5, page 22

1. The loss <u>of time</u> will never be regained. (8)
   The *lost time* will never be regained. (7)
   We will never regain the lost time. (7)

2. John's manner <u>of speaking</u> bored the audience. (7)
    John's *speaking manner* bored the audience. (6)

3. The quarterback was the leader<u> of the team</u>. (8)
    The quarterback was the *team leader*. (6)

4. Nocturnal animals avoid the light <u>of day</u>. (7)
    Nocturnal animals avoid *daylight*. (4)

5. The famous adventurer now craved a <u>life of calm</u>. (9)
    The famous adventurer now craved a *calm life*. (8)

6. What to eat for lunch was the problem <u>of the day</u>. (11)
    What to eat for lunch was the *daily problem*. (9)

7. Living <u>in a life</u> <u>of luxury</u> had become second nature to the
    wealthy family. (14)
    Living a *luxurious life* had become second nature to the
    wealthy family. (12)

8. The response <u>of the class</u> to the teacher's joke was many
    groans. (12)
    The class's response to the teacher's joke was many groans.
    (10)

Set # 6, page 25

1. The teacher's instructions were misunderstood <u>by the
    students</u>. (8)
    The students misunderstood the teacher's instructions. (6)

2. His success was resented <u>by his teammates</u>. (7)
    His teammates resented his success. (5)

3. The grocery store was operated <u>under new management</u>. (8)
    New management operated the grocery store. (5)

4. The grounds were observed <u>by means of hidden cameras</u>. (9)
    Hidden cameras observed the grounds. (5)

5. The last four games were lost <u>by the team</u>. (9)
    The team lost the last four games. (7)

6. The unusual plants were studied <u>by the scientists</u>. (8)
   The scientists studied the unusual plants. (6)

7. The touchdown pass was caught <u>by the speedy receiver</u>. (9)
   The speedy receiver caught the touchdown pass. (7)

8. The dance troupe was started <u>by a world-renowned dancer</u>. (10)
   A world-renowned dancer started the dance troupe. (8)

9. Their desire <u>for adventure</u> was tempered <u>by the rough seas</u>. (10)
   The rough seas tempered their desire for adventure. (8)

Set # 7, page 30

Below is one possible revision of the original submission. Notice that this excerpt is clearer, more direct, and more concise (189 words compared to 148 words).

Out There

Pluto and Uranus take turns being the most distant planets from the Sun. For years, scientists mistakenly hypothesized that Pluto was the most distant planet. While assimilating astronomical data, scientists learned their hypothesis was inaccurate. Fortunately, it is the scientist's nature to investigate all data. Based on the data, the astronomers learned that the two planets have intersecting orbits. While investigating, they also learned much about the two planets.

Scientists know that the surfaces of the planets are cold because they lack atmosphere and they are far from the Sun. It is the scientific community's dream to learn more about these planets. I just hope that we do not lose any lives attempting to realize this dream.

Should we be silent about this lurking danger? Notable scientists have silently pondered this very question. However, I am convinced that the public, not the scientific community, will answer this question.

Chapter Two

Set # 8, page 37

Claire

Claire <u>walked</u> (physical action) down the crowded school hallway on this first day of school. She <u>looked</u> (physical action) quickly to her left, and then to her right. Then, she <u>walked</u> (physical action) out and <u>joined</u> (physical action) the throng of students. Was anyone <u>watching</u> (physical action) her? Although she <u>wanted</u> (mental action) to look around, she kept <u>looking</u> (physical action) straight ahead. However, it <u>seemed</u> (mental action) that none of her classmates <u>looked</u> (physical action) at her as they quickly <u>walked</u> (physical action) to their classes.

Set # 9, page 44

Claire

Claire <u>trudged</u> down the crowded school hallway on this first day of school. She <u>glanced</u> to her left, and then to her right. Then, she <u>walked</u> out and <u>blended</u> into the throng of students. Was anyone <u>watching</u> her? Although she wanted to look around, she kept <u>staring</u> straight ahead. However, it seemed that none of her classmates <u>noticed</u> her as they quickly walked to their classes.

Set # 10, page 47

The General Store

The sun <u>shone</u> brightly in the sky; its hot summer heat <u>made</u> us tired and thirsty. We <u>continued</u> until we <u>came</u> to a small country store. We <u>walked</u> in and <u>saw</u> an old man behind the counter. He <u>had</u> a strange look in his eyes. Concerned, we <u>turned</u> around and <u>went</u> out the door. A cloud of dust <u>formed</u> behind us. (61)

The General Store

The hot summer heat *parched* our throats. We *trudged* along until we came to small country store. We *staggered* in and *noticed* an old man behind the counter who *glared* at us. Frightened, we *spun* around and *raced* out the door. A cloud of dust *billowed* behind us. (48)

Set # 11, page 50

As companies in practically every industry *rush* to sell their goods and services on the Internet, life *deteriorates* for those businesses that *languish*. Internet sales sites are *proliferating* and it seems that every business will soon own one. These companies *venturing* into cyberspace must *confront* a myriad of problems before they can *reap* the benefits of e-commerce. Companies will be *challenged* and *rewarded* in proportion to how they *embrace* the Internet.

Set # 12, page 52

1. The bank robber *revealed* his place for hiding the stolen money.

2. The crew *constructed* the building in less than six months.

3. I *contemplated* joining the circus as I walked around under the big top.

4. Unaware that Marty was *eavesdropping*, Grace and Ann talked about the surprise party they were planning for him.

5. In the summertime, I devour dozens of apples.

6. I *hustled* about the house as I tried to prepare for the party.

7. The boys spent all day *gawking* at the cute girls.

8. The politicians *debated* for hours about what was the proper course of action.

9. Jim *craved* an ice cream bar all day.

10. The art exhibit *proclaimed* that Picasso was greatest the artist of that era.

Set # 13, page 54

A Man's Best Friend

Since it was a very nice day, we decided to <u>slowly</u> <u>walk</u> through the park. A <u>briskly running</u> dog crossed our path in pursuit of a rubber ball. He <u>quickly took</u> the ball in his mouth and <u>swiftly walked</u> back to his owner. We could see the dog <u>breathing heavily</u> as he <u>abruptly placed</u> the ball at the man's feet. The man <u>roughly patted</u> the dog's head.

A Man's Best Friend

Since it was a very nice day, we decided to *stroll* through the park. A *speeding* dog crossed our path in pursuit of a rubber ball. He *snatched* the ball into his mouth and *trotted* back to his owner. We could see the dog *panting* as he *dropped* the ball at the man's feet. The man *rubbed* the dog's head.

Set # 14, page 55

Norman *barged* into the police station and *demanded* to talk with a police officer immediately. The sergeant sitting at the front desk *snapped* that he must wait his turn with the rest of the people. The sergeant's attitude *infuriated* Norman. He *wrapped* his hands around the sergeant's neck and *demanded* to *see* an officer. Within seconds, several officers *rushed* in and *arrested* Norman.

Chapter Three

Set # 15, page 66

1. The dog barked all day. (active voice)
   This sentence is written in the active voice because the verb, *barked*, describes the action of the subject, *dog*.

2. The dog ran after the fire truck. (active voice)
   This sentence is written in the active voice because the verb, *ran*, describes the action of the sentence's subject, *dog*.

3. The firemen were reprimanded by the mayor. (passive voice)
   This sentence is written in the passive voice because it contains a verb form of *to be* (*were*) and a past participle (*reprimanded*) that describe the action received by the subject, *the firemen*.

4. The championship trophy was won by the Cardinals. (passive voice)
   This sentence is written in the passive voice because it contains a verb form of *to be* (*were*) and a past participle (*won*) that describe the action received by the subject, *championship trophy*.

5. The girls sang loudly. (active voice)
   This sentence is written in the active voice because the verb, *sang*, is describing the action performed by the subject, *girls*.

6. The sisters had argued over the car for an entire week. (active voice)
   This sentence is written in the active voice because the sentence's verb, *had argued*, describes the action performed by the sentence's subject, *sisters*.

7. John had been away for a long time. (active voice)
   This sentence is written in the active voice because the sentence's verb, *had been*, describes the condition of the subject, *John*.

8. New York was selected by the committee as the site for its annual meeting. (passive voice)
   The sentence is written in the passive voice because the sentence's verb, *was selected*, describes the action performed by the sentence's main actor, *committee*.

9. The saxophone player received an encore. (active voice)
   The sentence is written in the active voice because the sentence's verb, *received*, describes the action performed by the sentence's subject, *saxophone player*.

10. The secretary is answering the telephone. (active voice)
    The sentence is written in the active voice because the sentence's verb, *is answering*, describes the action performed by the sentence's subject, *secretary*.

11. The football field was wet. (active voice)
    The sentence is written in the active voice because the sentence's verb, *was*, describes the condition of the sentence's subject, *football field*.

12. All occurrences of the passive voice were eliminated by the student writers. (passive voice)
This sentence is written in the passive voice because the sentence's verb, *were eliminated*, describes the action performed on the sentence's subject, *all occurrences*.

13. The violinist practiced every day. (active voice)
This sentence is written in the active voice because the sentence's verb, *practices*, describes the action performed by the subject, *violinist*.

14. The writing teacher was not pleased with the essays. (active voice)
This sentence is written in the active voice because the sentence's verb, *was not pleased*, describes the condition of the subject, *writing teacher*.

15. John stayed after class to meet with the teacher. (active voice)
This sentence is written in the active voice because the verbs of the sentence, *stayed* and *meet*, describe the action performed by the subject of the sentence, *John*.

16. Bob had stopped at every traffic light. (active voice)
This sentence is written in the active voice because the sentence's verb, *stopped*, describes the action performed by the subject of the sentence, *Bob*.

17. The compositions were returned by the teacher at the end of class. (passive voice)
This sentence is written in the passive voice because the verb of the sentence, *were returned*, describes the action performed on the subject of the sentence, *the compositions*.

Set # 16, page 69

1. The dog barked all day. (active voice)

2. The dog ran after the fire truck. (active voice)

3. The firemen were reprimanded by the mayor. (passive voice)

The mayor is the noun performing the action. Therefore, making *the mayor* the subject of the new sentence, the sentence rewritten in the active voice is: The mayor reprimanded the firemen.

4. The championship trophy was won by the Cardinals. (passive voice)
The Cardinals is the noun performing the action. Rewriting the sentence in the active voice, *the Cardinals* becomes the subject of the sentence: The Cardinals won the championship trophy.

5. The girls sang loudly. (active voice)

6. The sisters had argued over the car for an entire week. (active voice)

7. John had been away for a long time. (active voice)

8. New York was selected by the committee as the site for its annual meeting. (passive voice)
The committee is the action-performing noun of the sentence. To rewrite the sentence in the active voice, make *the committee* into the subject: The committee selected New York as the site for its annual meeting.

9. The saxophone player received an encore. (active voice)

10. The secretary is answering the telephone. (active voice)

11. The football field was wet. (active voice)

12. All occurrences of the passive voice were eliminated by the student writers. (passive voice)
The student writers is the action-performing noun in this sentence. To rewrite the sentence in the active voice, make *the student writers* the subject of the new sentence: The student writers eliminated all occurrences of the passive voice.

13. The violinist practiced every day. (active voice)

14. The writing teacher was not pleased with the essays. (active voice)

15. John stayed after class to meet with the professor. (active voice)

16. Bob had stopped at every traffic light. (active voice)

17. The compositions were returned by the professor at the end of class. (passive voice)
    The professor performs the action. To rewrite this sentence in the active voice, make *the professor* the subject: The professor returned the compositions at the end of class.

Set # 17, page 70

1. Threats were being issued throughout the tense ordeal. (passive voice)
   This sentence should remain in the passive voice because the author does not want to reveal the source of the threats.

2. The summit meeting had been convened. (passive voice)
   This sentence should remain in the passive voice because the writer apparently does not feel it is important to know who convened the summit.

3. The student council meeting was convened by Bob. (passive voice)
   This passive voice sentence should be rewritten in the active voice because the writer has revealed the performer of the action (*Bob*).

4. His fate had been foretold. (passive voice)

5. His fate had been foretold by the fortune-teller.
   This passive voice sentence should be rewritten in the active voice because the writer has revealed the performer of the action (*fortune-teller*).

6. The military secrets had been stolen. (passive voice)

This sentence should remain in the passive voice because the writer apparently does not want to reveal who stole the military secrets.

7. The spy stole the military secrets. (active voice)

8. The military secrets had been stolen by the spy. (passive voice)
   This passive voice sentence should be rewritten in the active voice because the writer has revealed who stole the military secrets (*the spy*).

9. Trash was being thrown all over the yard. (passive voice)
   This sentence should remain in the passive voice because the writer apparently does not feel it is important to know who was throwing the trash.

10. John threw trash all over the yard. (active voice)

Set # 18, page 72

1. The football game had been lost by the team.
   This sentence should be rewritten in the active voice because it is not clear that the *game* is more important than the *team*.

2. The queen was sighted by her loyal subjects.
   This sentence should remain in the passive voice because the *queen* is an important person relative to the *loyal subjects* in the sentence.

3. The hurricane was sighted by the terrified residents.
   This sentence should be rewritten in the active voice because *hurricane* is not clearly more important than the *terrified residents*.

4. The Super Bowl will be broadcast by Channel 2 in one week.
   This sentence should remain in the passive voice because the *Super Bowl* is an important event relative to *Channel 2* in the sentence.

5. The president will be interviewed by the newscaster.

This sentence should remain in the passive voice because the *president* is an important person relative to *the newscaster* in the sentence.

Set # 19, page 74

1. The band finished rehearsal and was given a well-deserved rest.
    This sentence is acceptable although it contains both an active voice verb (*finished*) and a passive voice verb (*was given*) because the writer has not shifted the sentence's subject.

2. As the king surveyed his empire, treachery was plotted by his enemies.
    This sentence is stilted because it contains an active voice verb (*surveyed*) and a passive voice verb (*was plotted*) and the writer has shifted the subject from *king* to *treachery*. A possible rewrite of the sentence is: As the king surveyed his empire, he was unaware of the treachery plotted by his enemies.

3. Before the campers left, the wolves had been heard howling in the woods.
    This sentence is stilted because it contains an active voice verb (*left*) and a passive voice verb (*had been heard*) and the writer has shifted the subject from *campers* to *wolves*. A possible rewrite of the sentence is: Before the campers left, they had heard the wolves howling in the woods.

4. The campers ventured into the woods and were attacked by wolves.
    This sentence is acceptable although it contains both an active voice verb (*ventured*) and a passive voice verb (*were attacked*) because the writer has not shifted the sentence's subject, *campers*.

5. The wolves ran away as the hunters were heard calling for help.
    This sentence is stilted because it contains an active voice verb (*ran*) and a passive voice verb (*were heard*) and the writer has shifted the subject from *wolves* to *hunters*. A pos-

sible rewrite of the sentence is: The wolves ran away when they heard the hunters calling for help.

Set # 20, page 75

Anna at the Science Fair

Anna worked all summer on her Science Fair presentation and was rewarded for her hard work. Her school selected her to represent it at the district Science Fair. Her experiment's innovation surprised her science teacher. At the Science Fair, the judges applauded Anna's findings as insightful. Later that day, her presentation was awarded the grand prize by the impressed judges. As she received her award, she saw her proud parents taking photographs. The Science Fair had been a tremendous success! (80)

Set # 21, page 77

Saturn

My colleagues and I, scientists from the University of California, analyzed the rings of Saturn. We have concluded that Saturn's rings are comprised of ice, frozen gasses, and rock particles. We intend to further study Saturn's rings because we want to understand the relationship between Saturn's rings and its moons. (50)

Chapter Four

Set # 22, page 84

1. The senator had no *recollection* of his campaign promise. Attaching the suffix, *-ion*, to the root verb, *recollect*, forms the nominalization.

2. The teacher's *reaction* to the news was a negative one. Attaching the suffix, *-ion*, to the root verb, *react*, forms the nominalization.

3. Each candidate is under *investigation* before his *nomination*.
   Attaching the suffix, *-ion*, to the root verb, *investigate*, forms the nominalization. Attaching the suffix, *-ion*, to the root verb, *nominate*, forms the second nominalization.

4. Many political prisoners have not had the benefit of _representation_ by counsel.
   Attaching the suffix, -_ion_, to the root verb, _represent_, forms the nominalization.

5. The _discussion_ of the class was on the field trip.
   Attaching the suffix, -_ion_, to the root verb, _discuss_, forms the nominalization.

6. The mayor's office started an _investigation_ into the council member's actions.
   Attaching the suffix, -_ion_, to the root verb, _investigate_, forms the nominalization.

7. The husband and wife made a _renewal_ of their wedding vows.
   Attaching the suffix, -_al_ to the root verb, _renew_, forms the nominalization.

8. The newspapers launched an _attack_ of a vicious nature at the candidate.
   The writer uses the verb, _attack_, as a noun in this sentence.

9. The _induction_ of the baseball player into the Hall of Fame took place on Friday.
   Attaching the suffix, -_ion_, to the root verb, _induct_, forms the nominalization.

10. Katie' s _reaction_ was predictable.
    Attaching the suffix, -_ion_, to the root verb, _react_, forms the nominalization.

11. Matthew made the _suggestion_ that we stop at the campsite.
    Attaching the suffix, -_ion_, to the root verb, _suggest_, forms the nominalization.

12. The editorial is a _reflection_ of the writer's thoughts.
    Attaching the suffix, -_ion_, to the root verb, _reflect_, forms the nominalization.

13. Bob's writing _improvement_ astounded everyone.

Attaching the suffix, -*ment*, to the root verb, *improve*, forms the nominalization.

14. The <u>*carelessness*</u> of his writing was apparent throughout the entire manuscript.
    Attaching the suffix, -*ness*, to the root adjective, *careless*, forms the nominalization.

15. The general signaled for a <u>*withdrawal*</u> of his troops.
    Attaching the suffix, -*al*, to the root verb, *withdraw*, forms the nominalization.

16. By your <u>*acceptance*</u> of this check, you agree to paint the house.
    Attaching the suffix, -*ance*, to the root verb, *accept*, forms the nominalization.

Set # 23, page 87

The nominalizations are italicized.

The English Teacher

The English teacher had little *expectation* that her class would attain improvement in their writing. There are few *indications* that her *assessment* of the situation should be under *reconsideration*. However, a *discussion* among the students yielded a different *conclusion* because they were unwilling to make an *acceptance* of her conclusion. It was their *decision* to have a *discussion* with the principal about the *replacement* of their teacher. They realized, nevertheless, that the principal would have a *reluctance* to accept their *suggestion*.

Set # 24, page 92

1. The admiration of the teacher by the class was apparent.
   (Situation No. 3: Nominalization is the subject of a weak verb)

2. Our consideration of the matter is that it is unimportant.
   (Situation No. 3: Nominalization is the subject of a weak verb)

3. Recognition and acceptance of a problem is the first step toward solving it. (Situation No. 4: Consecutive nominalizations)

4. Our solution to the problem is important to us. (Situation No. 3: Nominalization is the subject of a weak verb)

5. The boys have no remembrance of their misdeed. (Situation No. 2: Nominalization follows a weak verb)

6. There is recognition of the player's effort. (Situation No. 2: Nominalization inserted after an expletive)

7. The coach has come to the conclusion that his efforts are in vain. (Situation No. 1: Nominalization trails a weak verb)

8. There has been no indication by the strikers that they are giving in. (Situation No. 2: Nominalization inserted after an expletive)

Set # 25, page 97

1. The senator could not *recollect* his campaign promise. (8)

2. The teacher *reacted* negatively to the news. (7)

3. Before being *nominated*, each candidate is *investigated*. (7)

4. Counsel has not represented many political prisoners. (7)

5. The class *discussed* the field trip. (6)

6. The mayor's office *investigated* the council member's actions. (8)

7. The husband and wife *renewed* their wedding vows. (8)

8. The newspapers viciously *attacked* the candidate. (6)

9. The Hall of Fame *inducted* the baseball player on Friday. (10)

10. Katie *reacted* predictably. (3)

11. Matthew *suggested* that we stop at the campsite. (8)

12. The editorial *reflected* the writer's thoughts. (6)

13. Bob's *improved* writing astounded everyone. (5)

14. The careless writing was apparent throughout the entire manuscript. (9)

15. The general signaled his troops to *withdraw*. (7)

16. By *accepting* this check, you agree to paint the house. (10)

Set # 26, page 99

Writing Well

I contend that writing well is a matter of learning a few simple techniques. Teachers will no longer accept students ignoring these techniques. Therefore, there is no need for you to accept poor writing skills. Nonetheless, I know that you are inclined to disagree. However, I do not state this without offering proof. Do as I suggest, and try these techniques for one month. If after one month, you do not improve, then seek help. (76)

Chapter Five

Set # 27, page 108

Good Writing Skills

Good writing skills must be learned. (Short declarative sentence) Writing skills are like any other skill. (Short declarative sentence) It is (expletive construction) well known that poor writers have improved their writing. There are (expletive construction) many examples at both the middle school and high school level. There are (expletive construction) some students who improve more than others. There is (expletive construction) hope for everyone, however.

It is (expletive construction) easy for students to improve their writing. I am one of those who improved. (short declarative sentence) There are (expletive construction) still times when I write poorly but

<u>they are</u> (expletive construction) not as numerous as before. <u>It is</u> (expletive construction) as a result of better writing that my grades have improved.

Set # 28, page 113

Summertime

Our family enjoys summer vacation. *Consequently*, we usually go on a long trip. (Consequence) My aunt lives in New Orleans, *and* we often travel to see her (Continuity), *although* sometimes she comes to our house *so that* we can go on a trip together. (Comparison and consequence) *For instance*, we went to the Grand Canyon last year, *and* we really enjoyed ourselves. (Reinforcement and continuity)

Set # 29, page 116

The Mascot

Our high school does not have a mascot, and *this* upset many of the students. *They* decided to run a contest to see who could select the best mascot. *This* turned into a disaster. Some students wanted a cute mascot *that* would show how friendly our school was. *This* was unacceptable to the basketball players. *These* players wanted the mascot to be ferocious looking. The principal had to end the contest, and *that* is why we still do not have a mascot.

Set # 30, page 118

The Modest Coach

I was surprised when the team won all of its games. *Who* would have expected them to win every game? Warren Pease, *who* has been the coach of the school for 15 years, gave the credit to the players. He has always avoided praising himself. *Where* else can you find a coach *who* would not take at least some credit?

Set # 31, page 125

Stress in Our Contemporary World

Eating and exercise habits affect a person's health. *However*, heredity plays a part in determining a person's longevity too. Some scientists believe stress affects a person's health, and *consequently*, they are trying to determine why people are under more stress today than they were a generation ago. *Furthermore*, they are also trying to find a way to alleviate that stress. I feel that stress grows as civilization progresses, *although* other researchers do not embrace my view.

Yet, they cannot disagree that there are more people in the world today than there ever have been. This is one cause for the increasing level of stress. *For instance*, information moves faster than it ever has, *and* there is also more of it. *Why is this important to our progress?*

How people and information interact will be important to our future because this will determine the quality of our progress. For example, studies show that we can be overloaded with information, and this makes people anxious, and even violent. *Therefore*, we should seek solutions to these problems.

Chapter Six

Set # 32, page 138

1. Angered by Tim, Joe slammed down the telephone. (8)

2. Very embarrassed to participate in class, Mary answered a question for the first time yesterday. (15)

3. Excited about learning at the beginning of the term, the students were bored by the end of the term. (19)

4. Very excited at the thought of receiving presents, Jason stayed up all night and was the first one in the living room on Christmas Day. (25)

5. Depending upon the weather, we will leave tomorrow if it is close to being pleasant. (15)

6. Waiting to be fed, the baby is sitting in his high chair. (12)

7. Removed from society, the hermit had little use for contemporary technological advances. (12)

8. Having just won the Kentucky Derby, the young jockey now set her sights on the prestigious Preakness. (17)

Set # 33, page 141

1. After playing their hearts out in the first game, the team continued to play that way throughout the season.

2. After working hard, I won first place in the writing competition.

3. Against his better judgment, he bought the sailboat.

4. With a very long dialogue scene, the protagonist and antagonist opened the play.

5. After his parents waved good-bye to their son, he raced off to enjoy his newfound freedom as a college student.

6. Under different circumstances, Mr. Jones may have voted for the challenger rather than the current mayor.

7. With her English teacher accompanying Sarah, they left for the meeting with the principal at two o'clock.

Set # 34, page 144

1. Mr. Martin is concerned about our writing skills, but he did not change his teaching style.

2. I want to listen to the music, but I can't because the baby is sleeping.

3. We went out to eat, and then we went to a movie.

4. The team put up a valiant fight, but they lost in the fourth quarter.

5. Bob and Helen decided to eat at the new restaurant, and they invited Ann.

6. We were angry at all the traffic, and we called the mayor's office.

7. Jason felt that both candidates were qualified, but he chose not to vote on Election Day.

8. Mary wanted to live in Boston, but she has never lived in the Northeast and has never been away from home.

Set # 35, page 146

1. I am taking English this semester; my sister, pre-algebra.

2. My brother lives in Alaska; I, Hawaii.

3. Cassandra earned an A on her essay; John and Marsha, Bs.

4. We are traveling to Iceland this spring; Bermuda, this winter.

Set # 36, page 148

Rachel had never given much thought about what she was going to do when she grew up, but she has now decided to become a writer. Creativity runs in her family. Her brother is a writer; her sister, a screenwriter. Mr. Stones, her English teacher, told her that she had a talent for writing. She responded by starting a writing journal, and now she is writing in it every day. Rachel is excited about writing a best-seller, but she knows that she must work very hard to accomplish this dream.

Chapter Seven

Set # 37, page 156

The following passage makes use of a one-word sentence contrasted against three long sentences (20, 20, and 24 words, respectively.)

Vote

Vote. Why do Americans no longer exercise a right that people in other countries are willing to die for to achieve? Have we become too complacent about our civic duty, or rather, have we become too cynical about our elected leaders? The answer to these questions lies in the heart of each American; only when we search our hearts will we reaffirm this wonderful right.

Set # 38, page 159

The following passage opens with a 27-word sentence. This long sentence is then followed by three sentences containing 5 words each.

Our Earth

Caring for the environment is the most important duty we humans have because if we neglect this duty, there will be nowhere left for us to go. The ancient Greeks knew this. The conquering Romans knew this. The Native Americans knew this.

Set # 39, page 161

Time and Money

Time is money. This simple statement was true one hundred years ago, and it is true today. People have come to realize that they can exchange the services they can provide for money for the goods and services they need. There, the logic is undeniable; the more time a person has, the more opportunity he or she has to create valuable services. Many people avoid wasting money; however, these same people will waste time in nonproductive endeavors.

Set # 40, page 164

1. On the subject of where to go on their class trip, the students argued the entire day.

2. By winning the last five games, the team surprised their coach.

3. In Mr. Greene's classroom, the students learned many of life's lessons.

4. Lovingly, the mother picked up her newborn baby.

5. Solving the problem can be done in a number of ways.

6. Climbing mountains and backpacking are what John lives for.

7. Upset that his story was not published, he quit writing.

8. Of everyone in the class, Martha is the best writer.

9. Discussing his travels abroad, the guest speaker pleased the students with his stories.

10. In less than 20 minutes, John had written the paper that earned him an A.

Set # 41, page 168

Timing

Have you ever noticed how teachers always pick the worst times to assign projects and papers? My birthday is next week, and my parents want to throw a party for me.

My mother asked sweetly, "Why don't you invite some of your friends? But not more than six," she quickly added, as if ordering cupcakes.

I was so excited! I couldn't wait to go to school tomorrow.

The next morning, I raced into school and found my friends standing outside of our English teacher, Ms. Erickson's room. They didn't look very happy.

"Will you come to my party Saturday?" I asked the frowning group.

"We can't!" they screamed in unison. "We'll be working through the weekend on our English project."

I had completely forgotten about it. Guess what I'll be doing this weekend?

Set # 42, page 170

Notice how the second paragraph contrasts with the first paragraph full of long sentences.

Why Education?

Education provides the framework of our individual liberty. This is not just my opinion, but an everyday fact. It is so important for our children to learn the value of their education. Without education, they will never be able to realize their full potential.

Knowledge is power.

Set # 43, page 171

Stranded

Finally! This week of school was over! I was now planning a well-deserved weekend. My best friend, Frank, wanted me to go with him to the beach. His brother was going to take us there in his 1989 Toyota, he told me.

"Can his car even make it all the way across town?" I asked him.

"It can make it to the beach, but don't ask me about bringing us back."

Being stranded on the white beaches of Florida doesn't sound all that bad.

Chapter Eight

Set # 44, page 178

1. We left <u>all together</u>.

2. From his tone of voice, I <u>inferred</u> that he was upset and angry.

3. How do the clouds <u>affect</u> the temperature?

4. I felt <u>altogether</u> out of place at the party on Saturday night.

5. The <u>inference</u> taken from the fact that there are no school buses in front of school is that we will not be going on the class trip.

6. The Boy Scouts were not <u>affected</u> by rain as they hiked through the hills of central Texas.

7. I am not <u>altogether</u> sure why we are here.

8. Are you <u>implying</u> that I write poorly?

9. Such a statement could have a serious, long-term <u>effect</u> on me.

Set # 45, page 183

1. The competition became so boring that the <u>disinterested</u> judge also soon became <u>uninterested</u>.

2. The dog <u>sat</u> on the car to keep warm.

3. I will just <u>lay</u> the blanket down over here.

4. <u>Lie</u> down on the bed in my room.

5. The Spirit Club arrived early to <u>set</u> up the refreshments for the pep rally.

6. John was <u>lying</u> asleep across the lab table.

7. <u>Sit</u> down!

8. My brother is always <u>lying</u> on the sofa.

9. The nurse had <u>laid</u> a blanket over the shivering patient.

10. John was so <u>uninterested</u> in the class that he fell asleep.

Set # 46, page 188

1. The <u>principal</u> reason we lost the game was my fumble at the one-yard line.

2. He had <u>fewer</u> bruises on his body than I did.

3. The author <u>who</u> wrote this book is very talented.

4. <u>Who</u> is your favorite author?

5. John, to <u>whom</u> I am related, is attending the class.

6. The <u>principal</u> always attended every football game.

7. The <u>least</u> amount of time will be wasted if we walk rather than wait for the bus.

Chapter Nine

Set # 47, page 199

1. The federal government historically has been the only government entity that has successfully implemented and enforced pollution control laws.

2. More than any other factor, the Internet is effectively closing the gap between races and genders.

3. Handgun manufacturers can never make their products safe enough to prevent hundreds of accidental shootings each year.

4. Asian educators attribute the success of their students to year-round schooling.

5. Teachers' unions are responsible for the lack of change in school subjects.

6. Sports have taken an unintended dangerous lead role in the lives of thousands of adolescents.

Set # 48, page 203

Problem No. 1

Topic: Who Should Take the Lead in Cleaning Up Polluted Air in Our Large Cities?

Proposition Statement: The federal government historically has been the only governmental entity that has successfully implemented and enforced pollution control laws.

Outline:

I.   Effectiveness of Federal Legislation

II.   Ineffectiveness of State Legislation

III. A Solution for the Future

Problem No. 2

Topic: Is the Internet Creating an Economic Divide?

Proposition Statement: More than any other factor, the Internet is effectively closing the gap between races and genders.

Outline:

I.   Brief History of the Internet

II.   Why and How the Internet Is Bringing Us Together Socially

III. How This Unification Is Closing the Earnings Gap

Problem No. 3

Topic: Handguns Should Be Banned in the United States.

Proposition Statement: Handgun manufacturers can never make their products safe enough to prevent hundreds of accidental shootings each year.

Outline:

I.   The Deadly Statistics

II.   Gun Manufacturers' Admissions

III. The Only Real Solution

Problem No. 4

Topic: Should Schools Be in Session All Year?

Proposition Statement: Asian educators attribute the success of their students to year-round schooling.

Outline:

   I.   Asian vs. American Students

   II.   Why Asia Goes Year-Round

   III.   Are American Students Different?

Problem No. 5

Topic: Have School Subjects Become Outdated?

Proposition Statement: Teachers' unions are responsible for the lack of change in school subjects.

Outline

   I.   A Look at School Subjects: Then and Now

   II.   Teachers' Unions and Change

   III.   Is Change Good, However?

Problem No. 6

Topic: The Role of Sports in the United States

Proposition Statement: Sports have taken an unintended dangerous lead role in the lives of thousands of adolescents.

Outline:

   I.   Sports Instead of Learning

   II.   Why Such an Attraction? Why So Dangerous?

   III.   It's Not Just the Boys Now

Set # 49, page 207

1.   Smith, Pamela. *The Life and Times of an English Teacher.* New York: Random House, 1998.

2. Saunders, John. "Teaching Is My Life." *American Teacher Magazine*, 18 June 1999: 45–49.

3. Ramsey, Nancy. Interview by (author). Dover, Md., 1 December 2000.

4. Freeman, Jayne. "How to Teach English Literature." National Middle School Teachers of America, 30 November 1999: Available at: (state web address).

INDEX

Really. This isn't going to hurt at all . . .

Barron's *Painless* titles are perfect ways to show kids in middle school that learning really doesn't hurt. They'll even discover that grammar, algebra, and other subjects that many of them consider boring can become fascinating— and yes, even fun! The trick is in the presentation: clear instruction, taking details one step at a time, adding a light and humorous touch, and sprinkling in some brain-tickler puzzles that are both challenging and entertaining to solve.

Each book: Paperback, approx. 224 pp., $8.95–$10.95, Canada $11.95–$15.50

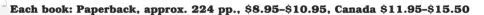

Painless Algebra
Lynette Long, Ph.D.
ISBN 0-7641-0676-7

Painless American History
Curt Lader
ISBN 0-7641-0620-1

Painless Fractions
Alyece Cummings
ISBN 0-7641-0445-4

Painless Geometry
Lynette Long, Ph.D.
ISBN 0-7641-1773-4

Painless Grammar
Rebecca S. Elliott, Ph.D.
ISBN 0-8120-9781-5

Painless Math Word Problems
Marcie Abramson, B.S., Ed.M.
ISBN 0-7641-1533-2

Painless Poetry
Mary Elizabeth
ISBN 0-7641-1614-2

Painless Research Projects
*Rebecca S. Elliott, Ph.D.,
and James Elliott, M.A.*
ISBN 0-7641-0297-4

Painless Science Projects
Faith Hickman Brynie, Ph.D.
ISBN 0-7641-0595-7

Painless Speaking
Mary Elizabeth
ISBN 0-7641-2147-2

Painless Spelling
Mary Elizabeth
ISBN 0-7641-0567-1

Painless Writing
Jeffrey Strausser
ISBN 0-7641-1810-2

Prices subject to change without notice. Books may be purchased at your local bookstore, or by mail from Barron's. Enclose check or money order for total amount plus sales tax where applicable and 18% for shipping and handling ($5.95 minimum).

Barron's Educational Series, Inc.
250 Wireless Boulevard, Hauppauge, NY 11788
In Canada: Georgetown Book Warehouse
34 Armstrong Avenue, Georgetown, Ont. L7G 4R9
Visit our website @ www.barronseduc.com

(#79) 4/03